# Optidynamics

## The Survival Theory
## for Companies
## in a World of Chaos

Steve Bevilacqua

ISBN: 979-8-9939913-0

# Table of Contents

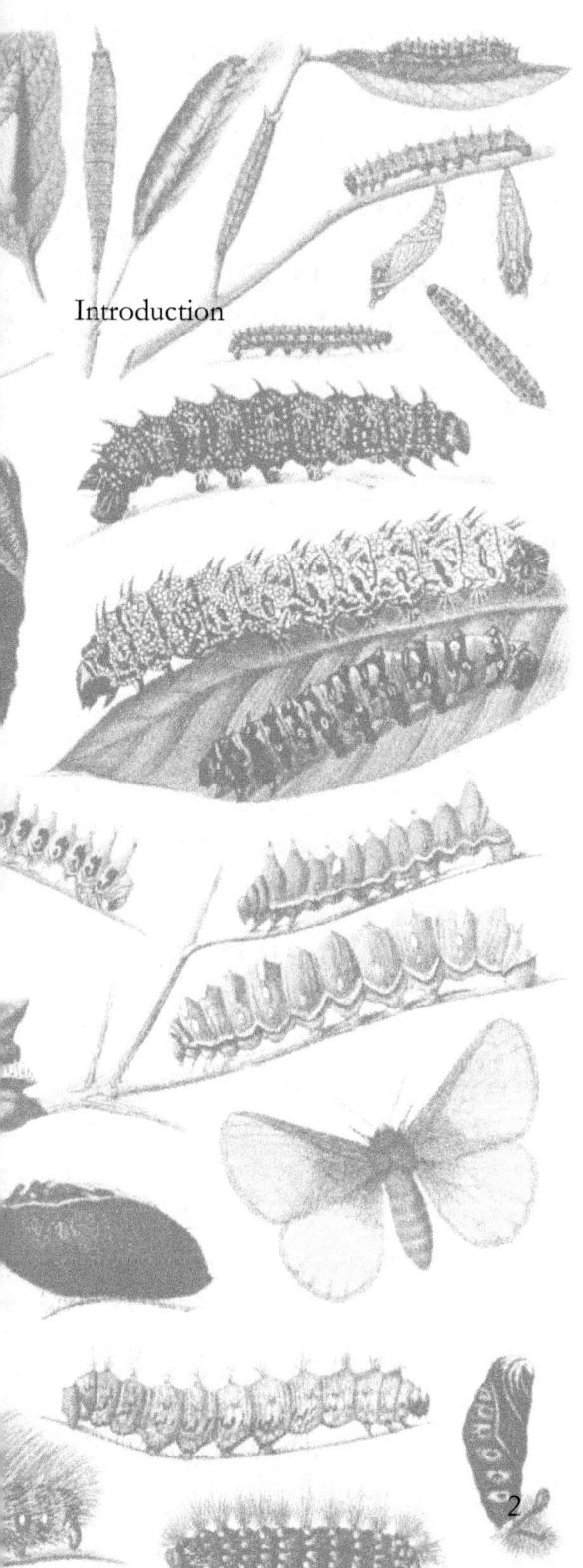

Introduction

It was a perfect Atlanta afternoon. I had just wrapped up a long and complex project with a small team. As my colleague and I walked past the parking deck toward a shopping plaza for lunch, I felt the weight of completion settle in. The project wasn't perfect, but it was solid. It would propel the company forward. I casually said to my colleague, "You know, I'm proud of what we did. It's pretty good."

He didn't hesitate. "It's better than good. It's done."

That moment shifted my thinking forever. I realized that I had been trapped in a cycle of perfectionism, endlessly refining ideas, convincing myself they needed to be bigger, better, and more groundbreaking before they were worth completing or even starting. In reality, the greatest enemy of my success wasn't failure, it was inertia.

That single sentence sparked a realization that what I had just experienced wasn't unique to me; it was universal. Every stalled project, every half-finished plan, every moment of hesitation is governed by the same invisible force that drags all systems toward disorder. That's when I began to see business not just as a collection of goals, teams, and deadlines, but as a living system subject to the same laws that govern the physical world. If science could explain why stars burn out and why energy fades without renewal, perhaps it could also explain, at least on some level, why ideas die, organizations slow, and execution loses momentum.

Every business, every project, every great idea faces a force of resistance that is invisible yet relentless, *entropy*. The concept of entropy, borrowed from thermodynamics, describes the natural tendency of systems to move toward disorder unless energy is applied to maintain that order. In business, this means that no matter how brilliant an idea is, if it isn't actively moved toward execution, it will decay into nothingness.

If you've ever had a groundbreaking idea that never made it off the drawing board, if you've watched promising projects stall, or if you've seen companies with boundless potential collapse under their own complexity, you have experienced the destructive pull of entropy.

Optidynamics is the concept of optimizing energy and execution to reduce entropy in business. It provides a framework for translating ideas into action by balancing three critical forces: energy, work, and entropy.

However, Optidynamics is about more than just finishing projects. It's about making the right investments of energy and effort intentionality to ensure that a business doesn't just survive but thrives over time. It applies scientific principles to business longevity, ensuring that entropy doesn't erode innovation, efficiency, and execution.

I've spent my career optimizing content operations, project execution, and digital transformation initiatives for some of the most recognizable brands on the globe. I've seen what works, and more importantly, I've seen what doesn't. I've watched businesses with brilliant ideas collapse under their own inefficiency, and I've helped companies streamline operations to break free from stagnation. When I began to formulate the concept of Optidynamics I was first driven by the thought of helping others whose ideas never got off the drawing board. I wanted to provide people with a framework to ensure that their efforts weren't wasted and their visions didn't decay into chaos. But it grew into something much larger as I realized it went beyond that single idea to a system capable of explaining and ensuring the long-time success of not just an idea but an entire company.

By the time you finish this book, you will understand why businesses fail due to unchecked entropy and how to prevent it. You will learn how to recognize, identify, measure and manage energy within your organization, develop systems to execute ideas efficiently and sustainably, and gain the tools to keep your business dynamic, adaptive, and resistant to stagnation.

Every day you hesitate, entropy is growing. Every idea that remains unfinished is losing its structure. Every project stuck in limbo is costing you energy without delivering results. Waiting is not neutral, it's actively harmful. Optidynamics isn't just a theory, it's a call to action. If you don't take control of entropy, it will take control of you.

You are about to embark on a journey that will fundamentally change the way you view execution, efficiency, and business longevity. It's time to stop obsessing over perfection and start channeling energy into execution. It's time to stop watching great ideas decay and start making them realized and lasting.

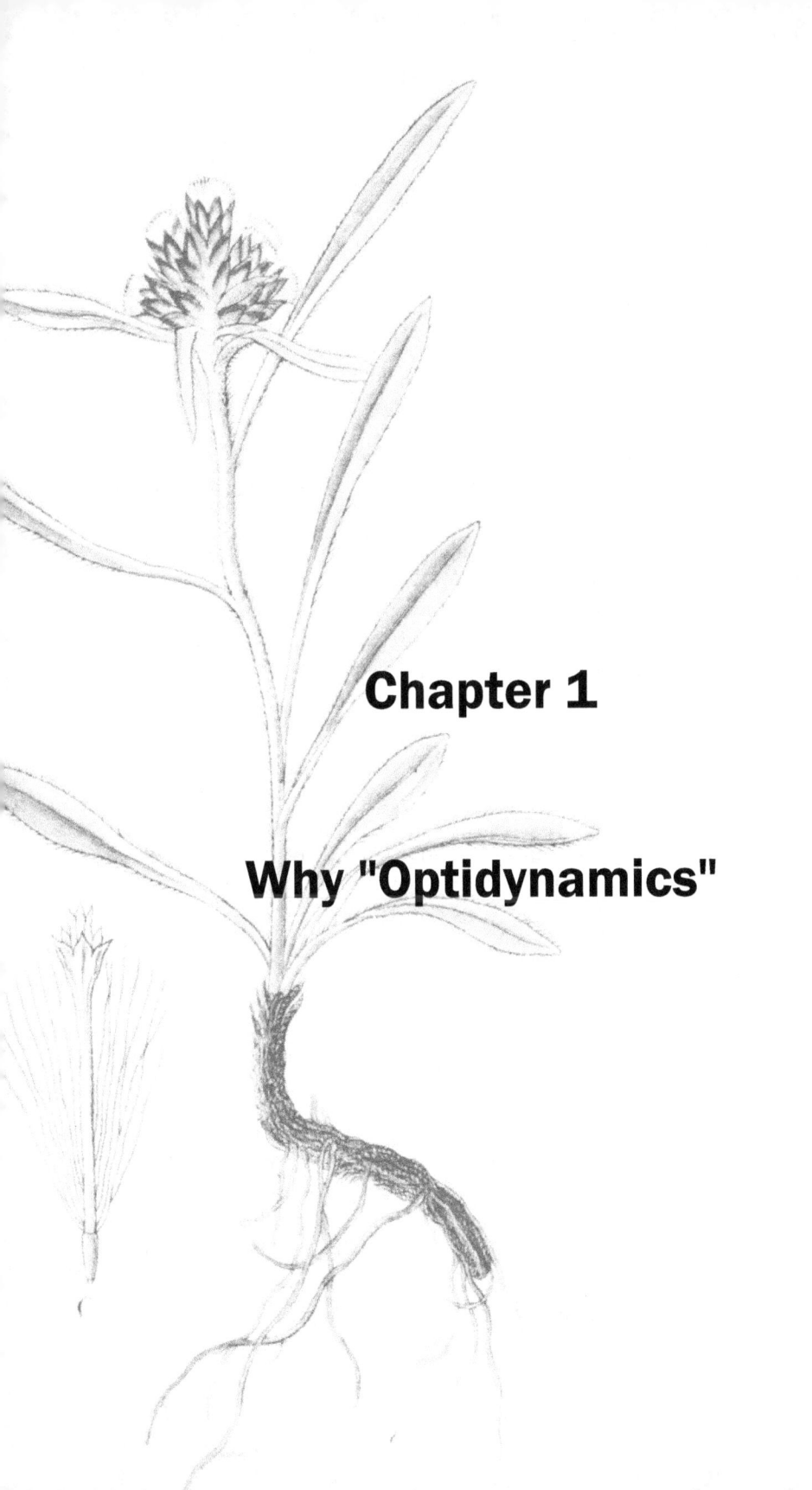

# Chapter 1

# Why "Optidynamics"

Names matter. They carry weight, intention, and meaning. When I set out to capture this framework in a single word, I knew it had to reflect both what it does and what it reveals.

Optidynamics wasn't chosen lightly. It's built from pieces that fit together like a puzzle, each one carrying its own story.

Let's start with "opti." It pulls double duty, and that's intentional.

First, there's the Latin side. "Optimus" means "best," the same root that gives us "optimum" and "optimization." When we talk about optimization, we're talking about making something work as well as it possibly can, squeezing out waste, finding the shortest path, using only the energy required. Nothing more, nothing less. In business terms, that means minimizing entropy and maximizing efficiency. It's the systematic pursuit of the best possible state for your organization, where resources, processes, and structures align to create the least friction and the most forward motion.

But "opti" has another origin, one that adds a different layer. From the Greek "optikos," derived from "opsis," meaning "sight" or "view." This is where we get words like "optic" and "optical." It's about vision, not just in the literal sense, but in the strategic sense. It's about seeing clearly where your business stands today and where it could go tomorrow. It's the kind of foresight that lets leaders cut through the fog of complexity and spot the path forward before anyone else does. Optidynamics isn't just about making things run better, it's about gaining the clarity to know *what* to make run better in the first place.

Two meanings wrapped into one prefix. Achieving the best, and seeing the way forward. Both essential, both interconnected.

Then there's "dynamics." part. This comes from the Greek "dynamis," meaning power, force, or strength. You see it in thermodynamics, the study of energy and its transformations on which this whole idea is inspired. Similarly, it's also in aerodynamics, biodynamics, psychodynamics. It's always about forces in motion, about how systems change and evolve over time. Dynamics isn't static. It doesn't sit still. It's the engine that drives transformation, the push and pull that keeps everything alive.

By weaving these roots together, *optimus* for achieving the best, *optikos* for clarity of vision, and *dynamis* for the forces that drive change, Optidynamics captures something bigger than any one of them alone. It's a framework that's both practical and visionary. Its goal is to provide a framework to optimize your business while keeping your eyes fixed on the horizon. It's about crafting systems that don't just run efficiently today but remain adaptable and resilient tomorrow.

In essence, Optidynamics means achieving optimal clarity by recognizing the forces of change.

That dual nature is what makes it powerful. Optidynamics aims to be a lens for understanding the deeper forces at work in every organization, and a method for shaping those forces to build something that lasts.

This name captures both a method and a mission. Now let's see how it transforms the way you view your organization.

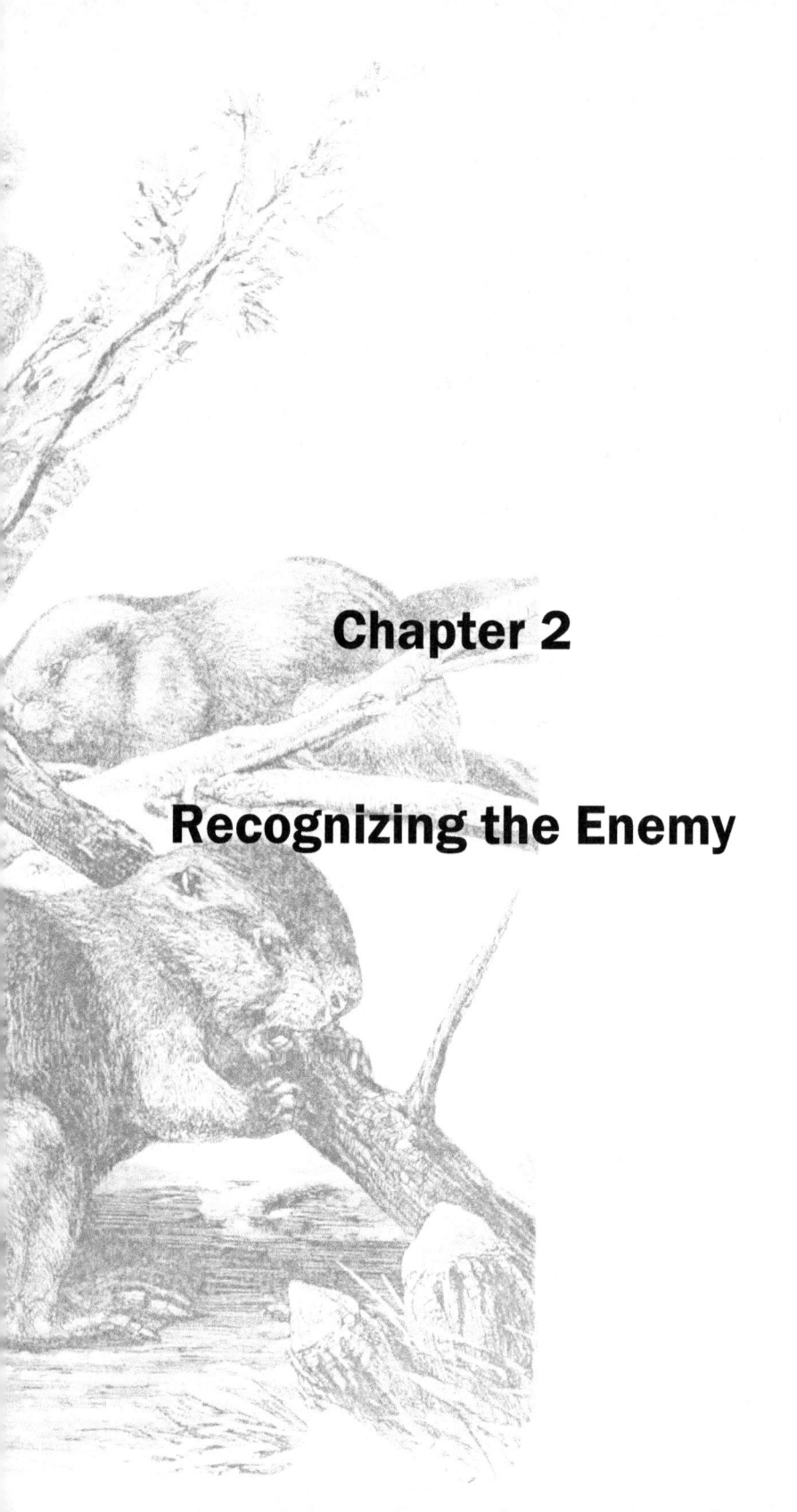

# Chapter 2

# Recognizing the Enemy

If you can accept entropy as the enemy of execution, then you're already beginning to see the invisible force that holds businesses back. Have you noticed great ideas in your own company fading before they even have a chance to succeed, what was once exciting potential beginning to crumble under inefficiencies? If so, you've already seen entropy at work. But entropy isn't just an abstract concept; it's measurable, predictable, and, most importantly, manageable. We'll break it down, not just in theory but in practical terms, using the very same principles that govern energy and disorder in the physical world. Understanding entropy is the first step to overcoming it, and that begins with redefining how we see energy, work, and the hidden costs of inaction.

The concept of entropy describes the tendency of systems to move toward disorder without external energy input. When applied metaphorically to ideas and their execution, we can think of an idea as a low-energy state, it's a concept that exists without much structure or form. Turning that idea into a finished product, however, requires overcoming this natural drift toward entropy, which demands energy, organization, and sustained effort.

In traditional thermodynamics, energy, work, and entropy are used to describe the transformation and flow of heat within physical systems. Optidynamics reimagines these same concepts to describe how businesses convert ideas into outcomes. Energy is the total available resources and organizational capacity such as time, talent, capital, creativity, and motivation. Work is the focused application of that energy toward specific outcomes, the productive effort that transforms potential into actual results. Entropy represents inefficiency, misalignment, and confusion that creeps into organizations as they scale or stagnate. This framework reveals important nuances about effectiveness. For instance, a highly skilled team, if mismatched to the task or lacking motivation, would be inefficient for the overall company, therefore adding to disorder and increasing entropy. So, it's not just about having these components, but about being focused in the right direction, and applying them with intention and clarity.

This reinterpretation helps us understand that having abundant energy (resources, talent, capital) is not enough. That capacity must be channeled through focused work that minimizes confusion and inefficiency. Only then can meaningful progress occur. Optidynamics provides a conceptual lens to assess how well an organization converts its available energy into productive work, not just how much potential it holds, but how effectively that potential is being transformed.

Let's examine the difference between energy and work more closely before moving forward. In Optidynamics, energy and work are closely related but distinct. Energy serves as the available capacity and resources, while work is the focused application of that capacity toward tangible results and specific goals. For a business to remain competitive and sustainable, it must consistently maintain and replenish its energy through talent acquisition, capital investment, innovation, and motivation, then channel that energy into productive work that reduces entropy and propels progress. Striking the right balance between these two forces is essential. Too much unused energy results in wasted potential, while too much work without adequate energy to sustain it leads to burnout.

Thus, the theory of Optidynamics suggests a company's ability to maintain healthy energy reserves while effectively converting that energy into meaningful work. Which is essential for minimizing entropy and achieving long-term success.

The relationship between energy, work, and entropy reveals why completion matters more than perfection. Every unfinished project represents potential energy trapped in a high-entropy state, while every completed project represents successful transformation of disorder into value.

But we are only in the starting blocks, as everyone who has tried and failed will know, there is a lot more to success than just the act of finishing. With the foundation laid for what Optidynamics represents, we can now turn our focus to the real adversary it was built to, if not defeat, at least understand and resist... entropy itself. So let's take a journey and see if a scientific principle discovered in 1860 and further refined around 1910 still has some more to teach us.

# Chapter 3

# Paralysis Through Analysis

Let's take a look at one more popular idiom that everyone in business is well aware of but can now be looked at through our new evolving lens. It also addresses the importance of completion but shows how the very act of overanalyzing can become an obstacle to execution.

While the previous chapter emphasized the necessity of finishing what we start, this chapter explores what happens when we struggle to even begin. This is where we confront a hidden form of entropy, mental stagnation. When we overthink, analyze endlessly, or hesitate in pursuit of the perfect decision, we aren't just delaying progress, we're allowing entropy to increase.

In thermodynamic terms, energy that should be directed toward forward motion instead gets consumed in a loop of endless refinement. Ideas stay trapped in the realm of potential, never materializing into real outcomes. The familiar phrase 'analysis paralysis' captures a truth that Optidynamics makes measurable. From our perspective, it's more than just indecision, it's a failure to convert energy into *usable* work.

Analysis paralysis increases the entropy and therefore the disorder of the process which could seem counterintuitive, as a good deal of energy is being used and put into the system. But instead of decreasing it through work, action, and progress, which would reduce entropy and bring the idea to completion, the individual, project or concept remains trapped in a loop of endless evaluation and reconsideration which increases mental and emotional entropy in the process. One may continually generate more options, hypotheses, and potential outcomes, but without ever narrowing the focus to take action. It's not enough to just consume energy to fight disorder, it must be done in a way that produces *useful*, not just "busy", work.

This idiom highlights the difference between simply having an idea and analyzing it endlessly or moving forward. It's only by doing, applying energy toward actual completion that you decrease the disorder or entropy. The longer you stay in a state of analysis, the less you're moving toward action, meaning you're stuck in a high-entropy state of indecision.

We use analysis paralysis as just one solid example of the opposite of useful work because it emphasizes a state of stagnation and disorganization. While it may seem like progress, as after all, analysis, planning, and discussion require effort and consume energy, not all work is of equal value. Just as a well-executed idea holds more worth than a poorly conceived one, the type of work being done matters. Simply expending energy is not enough. If you run as fast as you can in place you're not getting any closer to where you're trying to go. True progress comes from directing energy into structured, outcome-driven work, moving beyond analysis to action, where ideas take form and value is created.

Understanding how entropy operates internally, through indecision and overthinking, prepares us to take a deeper dive. It's time to build a more formal structure by learning the essential laws that govern every system, including your business.

# Chapter 4

# The Laws of Optidynamics

Let's explore a little of the fundamental laws of thermodynamics, the very principles that inspired Optidynamics. While this may seem like a step away from directly solving business challenges, it's a necessary foundation. Understanding these laws provides a lens through which we can examine the flow of energy, the nature of work, and the inevitable pull of entropy. Without this framework, the strategies that follow would lack the depth and theoretical grounding needed to be truly effective.

The laws of thermodynamics govern everything from the heat of the sun to the function of engines, and as we'll see, they also can serve as a foundation to explain why businesses thrive, stagnate, or collapse. By exploring these principles, we gain insight into how organizations accumulate disorder, why effort alone isn't enough to sustain success, and how the right balance of energy, execution, and structure can counteract entropy.

Though this chapter won't present a direct solution to a specific problem, it establishes the fundamental concepts that underpin everything that follows. In essence, this is the "why" behind Optidynamics, before we can optimize execution, we must first understand the nature of the forces at play.

### 1st Law of Optidynamics: The Conservation of Energy

"Energy cannot be created or destroyed, only transferred or transformed."

Think about boiling water on the stove. The electricity flowing into the pot, or the flame under it, is a type of energy. When the pot heats up, it transfers that energy into the water, raising the temperature. Some energy might escape as heat into the air, but all the energy is accounted for, it just changes form, from electricity to heat. No energy is lost, and none is magically created.

When you burn something like a log in a campfire, the energy stored in the wood is released as heat and light. The fuel combines with oxygen in the air, and the reaction creates the new substances of carbon dioxide, water and carbon. The total energy in the system, both before and after the reaction, stays the same. It simply shifts from being stored in the fuel to being released as heat and light.

In short, the First Law is about balance. Energy may look different after it's used, but it's never gone, it's just transformed. This principle helps explain everything from how engines work to why the sun shines. It's a reminder that energy is always part of the equation, even if it changes form.

In business terms, this means the available capacity (talent, resources, time, capital) required to bring an idea to life must come from somewhere and be carefully managed. Inspiration provides the initial spark of energy, but it must be transformed through structured work to reach completion. You can't expect an idea to materialize without applying focused work to overcome disorder and create value.

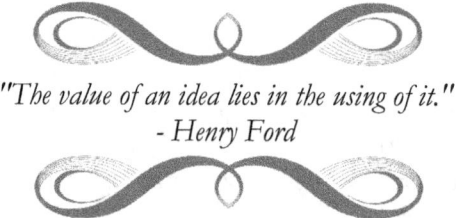

*"The value of an idea lies in the using of it."*
*- Henry Ford*

## 2nd Law of Optidynamics: Entropy Increases

"The entropy (disorder) of an isolated system will tend to increase over time."

The Second Law of Thermodynamics reveals the universality of what we discovered when the concept was first introduced. This isn't just a business phenomenon or a human tendency toward procrastination. It's a fundamental law governing everything from stars to startups. Energy naturally disperses, order naturally decays. No system, no matter how well-designed, is exempt.

Think about an ice cube sitting on a countertop at room temperature. It will melt, always and without exception, because heat flows from the warm room into the cold ice. This isn't a failure of the ice or poor ice design, it's physics. The same inevitability applies to your business – without continuous energy input, disorder isn't just likely, it's guaranteed.

This means accepting that degradation is the default state of your company. The question isn't whether entropy will affect your organization, but how actively you'll fight it. A room doesn't stay clean through good intentions. A project doesn't maintain momentum through initial enthusiasm alone. Only sustained, focused work keeps any system from its natural slide toward chaos.

*"Ideas are worth nothing unless executed. They are just a multiplier. Execution is worth millions." --Steve Jobs*

### 3rd Law of Optidynamics: From Temperature to Clarity

"The entropy of a perfect crystal at absolute zero is exactly equal to zero."

The Third Law of Thermodynamics states that as the temperature of a system approaches absolute zero, the entropy approaches a constant minimum value. In simpler terms, as things get colder and colder, approaching the coldest possible temperature, they become more and more ordered until they reach perfect crystalline structure with no disorder at all.

This law, unlike our first two, doesn't translate cleanly into business terminology. Temperature, as a metaphor, creates more confusion than clarity when applied to organizational dynamics. But this is precisely where Optidynamics reveals its strength as a creative framework rather than a rigid scientific translation. Optidynamics uses thermodynamic principles as creative inspiration, not literal scientific doctrine. The goal is to extract valuable insights about how organizations work, not to perfectly mirror every aspect of physics. Just as poets use metaphor to illuminate truth without claiming literal accuracy, business frameworks can borrow from science to reveal patterns and principles that might otherwise remain invisible.

Instead of forcing a temperature metaphor, we adapt this law to focus on what it really teaches us: the relationship between focus and clarity. We can reframe the Third Law as "Absolute Clarity", the principle that as systems become more organized and focused, disorder approaches its minimum possible state.

Using our new principle, we begin by thinking of a business idea in its rawest form. Like a gas, it's scattered and unstructured. At this stage, it's full of potential but lacks shape. As you refine it, putting in effort and energy to focus and develop it, the idea condenses, much like cooling a gas into a liquid and then into a solid. A solid idea is well-formed, structured, and actionable. It's more stable and organized than a loose, unfocused concept. And once an idea is in this state, its processes and procedures can be identified, documented, made repeatable and optimized.

The Third Law teaches us that maximum order requires maximum focus. Perfect crystallization in physics mirrors perfect clarity in business, and neither is fully achievable. The key insight is this: achieving a structured, low-entropy state, where processes run smoothly and ideas are fully realized, requires sustained energy input. It takes work to refine a chaotic brainstorm into a concrete plan, just as it takes energy to create crystalline order in physics. However, just as perfect crystals are rare and absolute zero is unreachable, no business can eliminate all disorder. There will always be some degree of unpredictability, shifting markets, or evolving challenges.

*"The will to win, the desire to succeed, the urge to reach your full potential... these are the keys that will unlock the door to personal excellence." – Confucius*

## *4th Law of Optidynamics: Maximum Entropy or the "Arrow of Time"*

The Fourth Law focuses on systems driven by external forces, emphasizing how energy and resources flow to maintain balance in an ever-changing environment. It's about how systems adapt over time, constantly fighting the natural drift toward chaos. The idea that processes naturally flow in one direction, from order to disorder, and cannot be reversed without external input is called "The Arrow of time"

When you pour a hot cup of coffee, it's out of equilibrium with the cooler surrounding air. Over time, heat flows from the coffee to the air until both reach the same temperature. This flow of heat explains the arrow of time, it moves in one direction, from hot to warm, spreading energy out. You can't reverse this process without external energy, like reheating the coffee.

This can be applied to incorporate the passage of time and the evolution of ideas. Without action, entropy increases, and the idea may never be realized. The natural course of time leads to ideas becoming outdated, irrelevant, or forgotten without execution. This is like the decay of materials such as the rusting of steel. If an idea is not acted upon, it fades into chaos, ambiguity, or neglect. A project that starts out as an exciting, organized concept could be abandoned, leading to a higher state of entropy.

Execution or delivery fights against this inevitable increase in entropy. Through consistent and focused work, the idea maintains its structure, reduces disorder, and has the potential to reach completion. The longer you leave an idea or any business challenge unaddressed, the more likely it's to lose its original clarity. But with consistent and correct use of energy and effort, you can steer the project toward completion, fighting the natural tendency for things to fall into disorder as time progresses.

*"The increase of disorder or entropy is what distinguishes the past from the future, giving a direction to time." - Stephen Hawking*

Together, these laws reveal a complete picture: Energy must be conserved and directed (First Law). Disorder naturally increases without intervention (Second Law). Perfect order requires perfect focus (Third Law). Time, and along with it disorder, flows in only one direction (Fourth Law). Understanding these principles transforms entropy from an invisible force into a manageable challenge

Now that we have the theoretical framework, let's see how these laws have played out in the real world, where companies either respected or ignored them, and either thrived or paid the price.

# Chapter 5

# Companies that Succumbed to Entropy

*Princes, this clay must be your bed, In spite of all your towers;*
*The tall, the wise, the reverend head Must lie as low as ours!*
*- Funeral Hymn, Isaac Watts*

Every dominant company follows a predictable pattern. They begin in a low-entropy state with clear vision, innovation, and agility. Over time, however, entropy increases through organizational complexity, resistance to change, and failure to adapt. Without sufficient work to reduce entropy and foster innovation, decline becomes inevitable. More agile competitors with lower entropy, capable of applying energy more efficiently, eventually displace them.

This is why no company retains dominance forever. As companies grow and age, internal entropy inevitably increases unless there is consistent, intelligent effort to adapt and evolve. Long-term success requires continuous innovation, maintained agility, and efficient energy application to meet new market demands.

Let's examine how this framework applies to well-known companies that failed to manage entropy and understand what they might have done differently.

An entire generation experienced the excitement of going into a Blockbuster and looking through the rows of colorful boxes, the smell of fresh popcorn in the air. Navigating the difficulty of trying to decide on the one movie their parents allowed them to rent, with the promise of "Be Kind - Please Rewind" or face the dreaded fees. Once the dominant force in home video rentals, Blockbuster failed to adapt to the rise of first, mail-delivered convenience, and later digital streaming and on-demand content. Netflix, an early competitor, recognized customer demands for convenience and flexibility, building a leaner and more energy-efficient operation. Blockbuster, on the other hand, ignored early opportunities to partner with Netflix and remained burdened by large retail overheads. Its rigid processes and outdated business model increased internal entropy, making it impossible to compete in the rapidly evolving market. In the end, the failure to manage increasing entropy led to Blockbuster's collapse, as Netflix and other digital platforms took its place. Think about your own company. Are you clinging to familiar ways while the market shifts around you, just as Blockbuster did?

Perhaps you got to experience the joy of snapping pictures on a Kodak disposable camera, waiting eagerly for the film to be developed, hoping that at least one shot turned out just right? For generations, Kodak was synonymous with photography. Even though it invented the first digital camera – ironically, it was digital photography that ultimately led to Kodak's downfall. The company resisted change, clinging to its profitable film business while competitors embraced the new technology. This decision-making paralysis, combined with the inability to restructure outdated processes, resulted in Kodak's market decline. Leadership failed to channel energy into innovation, allowing entropy to grow unchecked within its legacy systems. When it finally attempted to pivot, it was too late. Companies that had embraced digital photography early on had already captured the market, leaving Kodak behind.

There was a time when nearly everyone had a Nokia phone, indestructible, with a battery that seemed to last forever, and of course, Snake was the height of mobile gaming. Nokia was the global leader in mobile phones, yet it struggled to respond effectively to the emergence of smartphones. While Apple and Android embraced touchscreens and app ecosystems, Nokia clung to outdated operating systems and hardware designs. Internal coordination was weak, and there was little urgency in responding to market trends. As a result, Nokia's competitive energy eroded, and it lost its leadership position to companies that had kept entropy low and focused energy toward innovation. The company's decline illustrates how failing to address organizational disorder, such as internal silos and misaligned strategies, can sap a company's ability to compete and adapt.

Each of these companies failed to apply the principles of Optidynamics. They did not adequately manage entropy, leading to inefficiencies and rigid structures. They lacked the necessary energy input to innovate and remain competitive. Their organizational structures were ill-suited to adapt to changing environments. Meanwhile, their successors: video on demand, digital camera innovators, smartphone leaders, and new social platforms, kept entropy low, directed energy toward innovation, and maintained adaptable structures. These examples serve as a cautionary tale: without continuous effort to manage entropy, even the most dominant companies will eventually fall.

Failure is often easier to study than success. But to truly master Optidynamics, we must also understand what a few rare companies did right and how they kept entropy at bay for years and even centuries.

# Chapter 6

# Keeping Entropy in Check

*"An old pond — a frog jumps in, the sound of water."*
-(古池や蛙飛び込む水の音
- *Furu ike ya / kawazu tobikomu / mizu no oto)*

Having examined how companies fail, let's explore what we can learn from the longest lasting company ever, and then the longest lasting company in the United States. While entropy makes eventual decline inevitable, these examples show how the right strategies can delay that fate for centuries.

The oldest continuously operating company on record is Kongō Gumi, a Japanese temple builder founded in 578 CE.. Specializing in Buddhist temple construction, it operated continuously for over 1,400 years, offering fascinating insights into long-term entropy management.

Specialization in Buddhist temple construction played a key role in maintaining low entropy in Kongo Gumi's operations. By focusing exclusively on a niche industry, the company minimized the complexity and variation in its work. This specialization allowed the company to build a highly efficient structure with expertise in a particular craft, reducing the need for excessive energy or resources to diversify or adapt. The company didn't need to expend energy on complex diversification strategies; instead, it focused on maintaining excellence in a specific area. In Optidynamic terms, this constant focus on one core function helps reduce entropy because there is less systemic disorder created by frequent shifts in direction or operations.

One of the other primary ways Kongo Gumi reduced entropy was through effective leadership succession. The company was managed by successive generations of family leaders who ensured continuity in the company's values, practices, and operations. This leadership structure kept the company from fragmenting or experiencing the confusion that often arises when there is no clear leadership or when leadership changes frequently. In Optidynamic terms, continuous leadership is akin to maintaining low entropy because it ensures that the company's direction is always aligned, minimizing disorganization.

Kongo Gumi's corporate culture likely played a significant role in maintaining order and structure over centuries. The company had deeply ingrained traditions, values, and operational practices that were passed down through generations. This cultural continuity prevented the company from fragmenting or adopting conflicting operational methods, which would introduce disorder. From an entropy perspective, culture serves as an internal energy reserve that resists the disorienting effects of external or internal pressures. This cultural stability helped maintain a low-energy system that was self-sustaining over centuries.

Despite its focus on temple construction, Kongo Gumi adapted to changing external conditions, such as societal, political, and technological shifts. For instance, during times of war or societal upheaval, the company pivoted to projects that were still in line with its core expertise but suited to the current needs of society. This kind of adaptation to external entropy is important because it ensures that the company can continue to operate within changing environments. By investing energy into adapting to new conditions, Kongo Gumi ensured that its core structure and processes remained intact.

Kongo Gumi was also able to remain agile by evolving internal practices and incorporating new technologies and methodologies as needed. While it maintained its primary focus on temple construction, it did not shy away from adapting its tools and techniques to be more effective or efficient. Technological advancement and methodological shifts are energy inputs that help prevent the organization from becoming outdated and chaotic. These adaptations lowered the internal entropy by preventing stagnation and ensuring that the company could meet evolving needs and challenges.

Over the span of 1,400 years, Kongo Gumi didn't survive by standing still. It kept moving, kept adjusting, and most importantly, kept working. When the world around it changed, the company responded. Not with panic or overreaction, but with thoughtful energy. It trained new leaders, embraced innovation when needed, and never let itself drift too far from the work that gave it strength in the first place.

What made Kongo Gumi different was its unwavering focus. While other companies might have tried to do everything, it stuck to its core. It honed its craft, passed down its culture, and stayed grounded in what it knew best. This clarity prevented it from becoming bloated or disorganized, even as generations came and went.

Of course, there were moments when outside forces demanded change. The world shifted, expectations evolved, and pressure mounted. During those times, Kongo Gumi didn't resist reality. It poured energy into the right places, realigned with its purpose, and found ways to stay relevant without losing itself in the process.

That balance between tradition and evolution, between structure and the natural pull of disorder, is what kept the company alive. Through discipline, adaptability, and a clear sense of identity, Kongo Gumi showed that while no business can avoid chaos forever, the right moves at the right time can keep it away for a very long time..

Yet even Kongō Gumi's remarkable story carries a final, sobering lesson. During Japan's economic bubble in the 1980s, the company borrowed heavily to invest in real estate, stepping outside the disciplined focus that had sustained it for centuries. When the bubble burst, those assets collapsed in value, and as temple contributions declined through the late 1990s, debt compounded quietly for two decades. By 2006, the company could no longer service its obligations and was forced into liquidation, its operations absorbed by the Takamatsu Construction Group, where it continues today as a subsidiary still building temples. A company that survived wars, typhoons, and an entire government campaign to eradicate its industry was ultimately undone not by external chaos, but by a financial misstep that introduced entropy into the one area it had left unguarded. It is perhaps the purest proof that entropy never stops looking for a way in.

If Kongo Gumi teaches us about longevity across a millennium, our next example brings the lessons closer to home, showing how one American company has battled entropy for over two hundred years

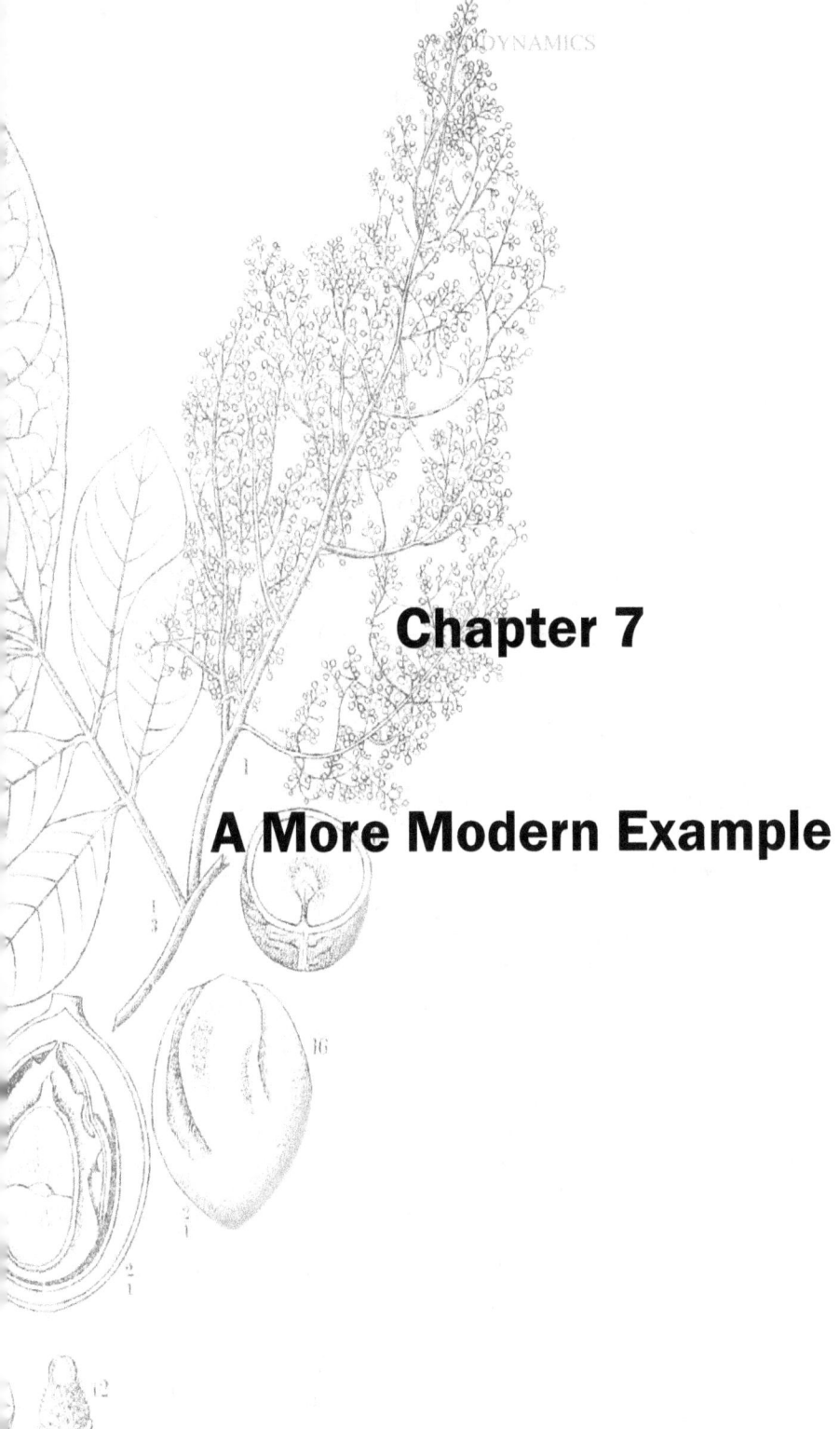

# Chapter 7

# A More Modern Example

In 1810, a group of merchants in Hartford, Connecticut, gathered to form a fire insurance company. At the time, fire was one of the greatest threats to homes and businesses, capable of destroying entire towns overnight. These merchants recognized a need for protection, to create an organized effort to manage risk and distribute the financial burden of catastrophe. What they built that year was more than just an insurance company; it was a system of stability in an era of uncertainty. More than two centuries later, The Hartford stands as one of America's longest-operating companies, with over 200 years of continuous operation, a testament to its ability to adapt, innovate, and resist the creeping forces of entropy that have swallowed so many of its competitors.

Businesses, much like physical systems, are constantly battling entropy, the slow accumulation of inefficiencies, redundancies, and missteps that, if left unchecked, lead to stagnation and decline. The Hartford has not only endured the natural drift toward disorder but has actively fought against it, injecting energy and strategy at key moments to maintain its competitive edge. This ability to counteract entropy was not accidental, but instead a product of deliberate actions, visionary leadership, and an organizational culture that values adaptation as a necessity rather than an occasional course correction.

Throughout its history, The Hartford has successfully navigated market disruptions and economic upheavals by consistently evolving its offerings. What began as a fire insurance provider grew to include life insurance, auto insurance, and employee benefits. At every stage, the company assessed its position, identified emerging risks, and adjusted its model to meet new demands. This adaptability is a prime example of how companies can minimize entropy by maintaining a focused yet flexible approach to their core business.

The company's leadership has also played a significant role in counteracting entropy. Unlike many organizations that succumb to bureaucratic inertia, The Hartford has consistently reinvigorated itself through strategic mergers and acquisitions. These moves injected new energy into the system, allowing the company to refresh its market position and stay relevant as industries evolved. The integration of new businesses into its structure required careful management of complexity, ensuring that acquisitions brought synergy rather than chaos. This balancing act is crucial in any long-standing company: too little change leads to obsolescence, while too much unchecked expansion breeds disorder.

One of the most effective ways The Hartford has managed entropy is through continuous feedback loops. Companies that fail to learn from their past mistakes are doomed to repeat them, but The Hartford has leveraged its historical knowledge to refine its operations. Whether responding to regulatory changes, economic downturns, or shifting customer needs, the company has demonstrated an ability to analyze, adjust, and improve. This process of iterative refinement ensures that disorder does not accumulate to unmanageable levels. This is not just an amazing technique for your company or business but is also something you can apply to your personal life with the same hope of success. When is the last time you took a moment to think about how your actions are affecting your life and how trying a small change or improvement may make a difference. Now what if you did this intentionally every day?

Using the Optidynamic framework, we can break down The Hartford's long-term success into measurable components. The company's initial vision and strategic focus provided a strong foundation, ensuring that all adaptations aligned with a central purpose, while the energy it has injected over the years through innovation, leadership transitions, and acquisitions has continuously offset the natural tendency toward entropy. By applying sustained effort in key areas, market adaptation, leadership structure, and operational efficiency, The Hartford has remained resilient despite the inevitable challenges that come with time.

Its story is one of longevity as well as a guideline for businesses seeking to defy entropy. You must realize and embrace the impossibility of avoiding disorder altogether. Rather, learn to recognize where disorder emerges and how to strategically apply energy to bring the system back into equilibrium. The Hartford's ability to survive for over 200 years is a testament to the power of this principle, proving that with the right balance of stability and evolution, a company can stand the test of time. This dynamic company shows how resilience can survive across centuries. Now, let's move to the modern age and see how one of the most dynamic companies of today, Alphabet, had to re-engineer itself to stay ahead of entropy's pull.

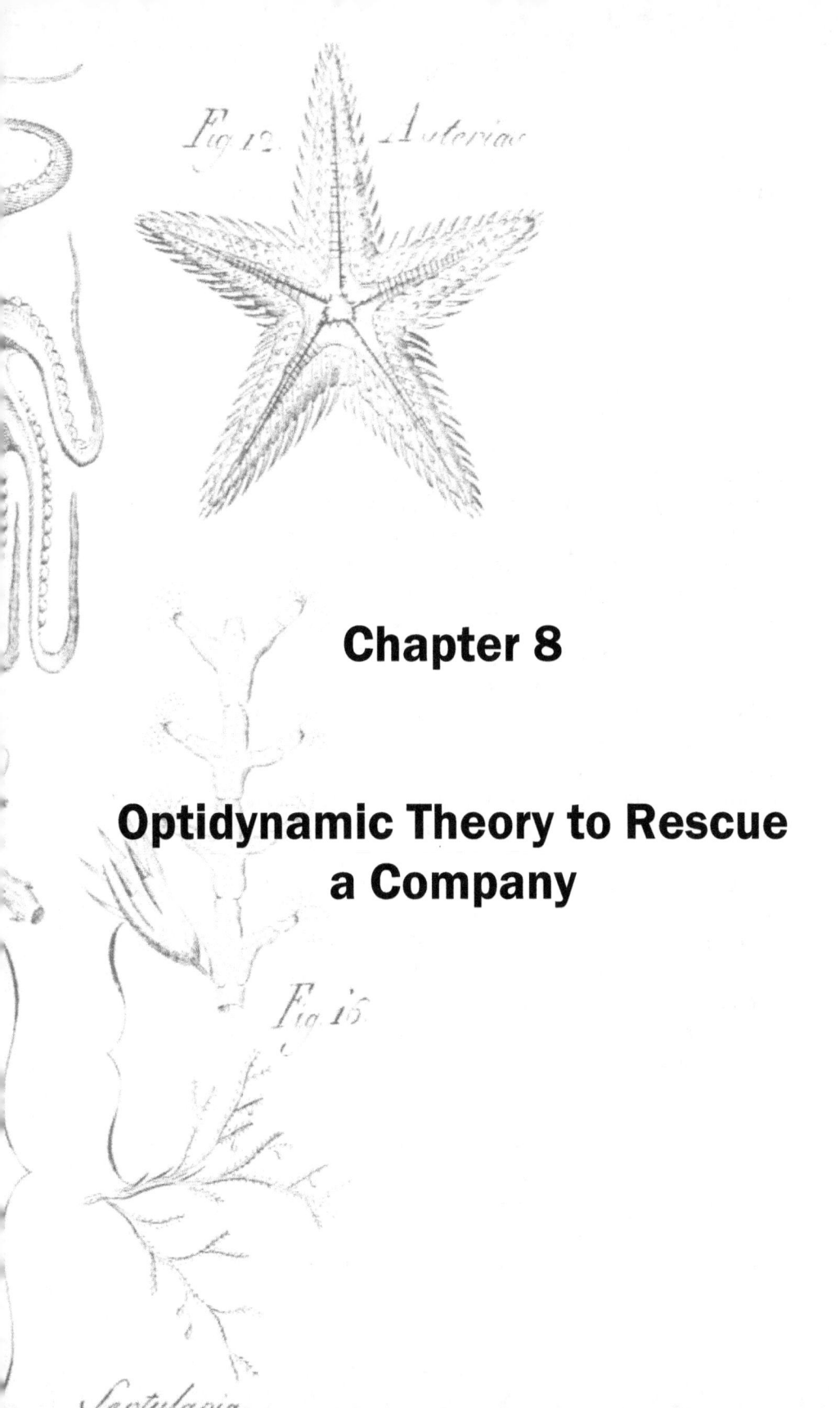

# Chapter 8

# Optidynamic Theory to Rescue a Company

We've examined companies that fell to entropy and those that resisted it across centuries. Now let's see how these principles apply to a modern company that restructured itself specifically to fight disorder. And how this method can be leveraged to rescue a company that is currently at risk due to enormous growth by lowering entropy and therefore granting the company energy to fight another day.

In 1998, two Stanford PhD students, Larry Page and Sergey Brin, developed a search engine in their dorm room. Their mission was simple yet ambitious: to organize the world's information and make it universally accessible and useful. That search engine, Google, became the cornerstone of a company that would redefine the Internet. But as their ambitions grew beyond search, Google faced a challenge that threatens every successful enterprise, complexity. By 2015, the company had expanded far beyond search into advertising, artificial intelligence, cloud computing, hardware, self-driving cars, and even life sciences, all managed within a single entity. The sprawl created confusion, slow decision-making, and diluted its focus. Instead of allowing entropy to take hold, the company executed a bold move, restructuring itself into Alphabet Inc. A holding company that allowed its various ventures to operate with more autonomy while maintaining a shared strategic direction. This decision wasn't just corporate rebranding; it was a calculated effort to manage entropy and sustain long-term innovation.

Alphabet's continued success, just like that of The Hartford and Kongo Gumi, is best understood through the principles of Optidynamics. Businesses, like physical systems, tend toward entropy. The more they grow, the more complexity they accumulate. Without deliberate effort, that complexity can lead to stagnation. Alphabet has countered this through continuous injections of energy, whether through innovation, acquisitions, or restructuring, in order to keep its focus sharp and its operations efficient.

Its initial mission provided a solid foundation and clear direction, but as complexity increases with growth, the company strategically applied energy to stay agile. However, as Alphabet expanded, the increasing number of projects and business units introduced entropy into the system. More teams, more technologies, and more markets meant a growing risk of fragmentation. Recognizing this, they applied significant and directed energy to maintain order. The 2015 restructuring was a planned effort to reduce entropy, creating independent entities like Waymo, Verily, and DeepMind. This modular approach ensured that each venture could pursue its goals without adding any excessive complexity to the fundamental core operations of Google.

By granting each subsidiary operational independence, Alphabet created smaller and more focused systems with their own energy sources and feedback loops. This separation localized and reduced entropy which prevented disorder in one division from spreading across the entire organization. Each entity could apply its energy more efficiently toward its unique objectives, maintaining clarity of purpose and reducing internal friction. In Optidynamic terms, Alphabet reduced systemic disorder by segmenting complexity into manageable and self-correcting units, allowing each part of the whole to operate with greater stability and adaptability

Their ability to manage entropy isn't just about its structure, it's also about its approach to innovation. The company has consistently channeled energy into acquiring and integrating new businesses while ensuring that they contribute meaningfully to its larger ecosystem. Acquisitions like YouTube, Android, Nest, and Fitbit weren't just about expansion; they were strategic investments that reinforced Alphabet's core strengths. By carefully integrating these businesses rather than allowing them to create unchecked disorder, Alphabet maintained a dynamic yet controlled system.

Another key factor in Alphabet's entropy management is, as we have seen with other successful companies, its use of feedback loops. Unlike companies that stagnate due to rigid hierarchies, Alphabet fosters a culture of iteration and refinement. Products like Google Search and YouTube continuously evolve based on data-driven insights, keeping them relevant and competitive. These feedback mechanisms act as stabilizing forces, ensuring that the company doesn't drift into inefficiency. What feedback loops could you deploy to ensure with growth comes improvement?

Using the Optidynamic framework, we can see how Alphabet has maintained its dominance. Its initial mission provided a solid foundation and clear direction, but as entropy increases with growth, the company strategically applied energy to stay agile. The restructuring into Alphabet, the integration of acquisitions, and the iterative improvement of its core products all demonstrate a commitment to reducing disorder while sustaining innovation.

However, the Alphabet restructuring also introduced new challenges that illustrate entropy's persistent nature. Managing a diverse portfolio of independent companies requires sophisticated coordination mechanisms that can themselves become sources of complexity. The parent company must balance autonomy with strategic alignment, ensuring that Waymo's innovations complement Google's ecosystem without stifling either unit's independence.

Additionally, the model creates potential resource allocation dilemmas. When multiple subsidiaries compete for talent, capital, or leadership attention, internal friction can emerge. Critics have noted that some Alphabet ventures have struggled to achieve the scale and impact initially envisioned, suggesting that structural solutions alone cannot guarantee innovation success.

The Alphabet approach also faces the ongoing challenge of maintaining entrepreneurial culture within increasingly large organizations. As individual units mature, they risk developing their own internal entropy, recreating the very problems the restructuring was designed to solve. This highlights a key Optidynamics insight: entropy management is never a one-time fix but an ongoing discipline.

This story is a powerful lesson in entropy management. Companies don't fail because they grow; they fail because they don't manage the disorder that comes with growth. Alphabet's proactive approach and its willingness to restructure, adapt, and reinvest in its future, has allowed it to remain one of the world's most influential companies.

By understanding and applying the principles of Optidynamics, other businesses can learn how to sustain their momentum, keeping entropy in check while driving innovation forward. We see that even the most innovative companies must actively fight entropy to stay sharp. Now that we've seen how these forces play out in the real world, it's time to turn the lens onto your own organization and explore practical ways to reduce entropy before it can take hold.

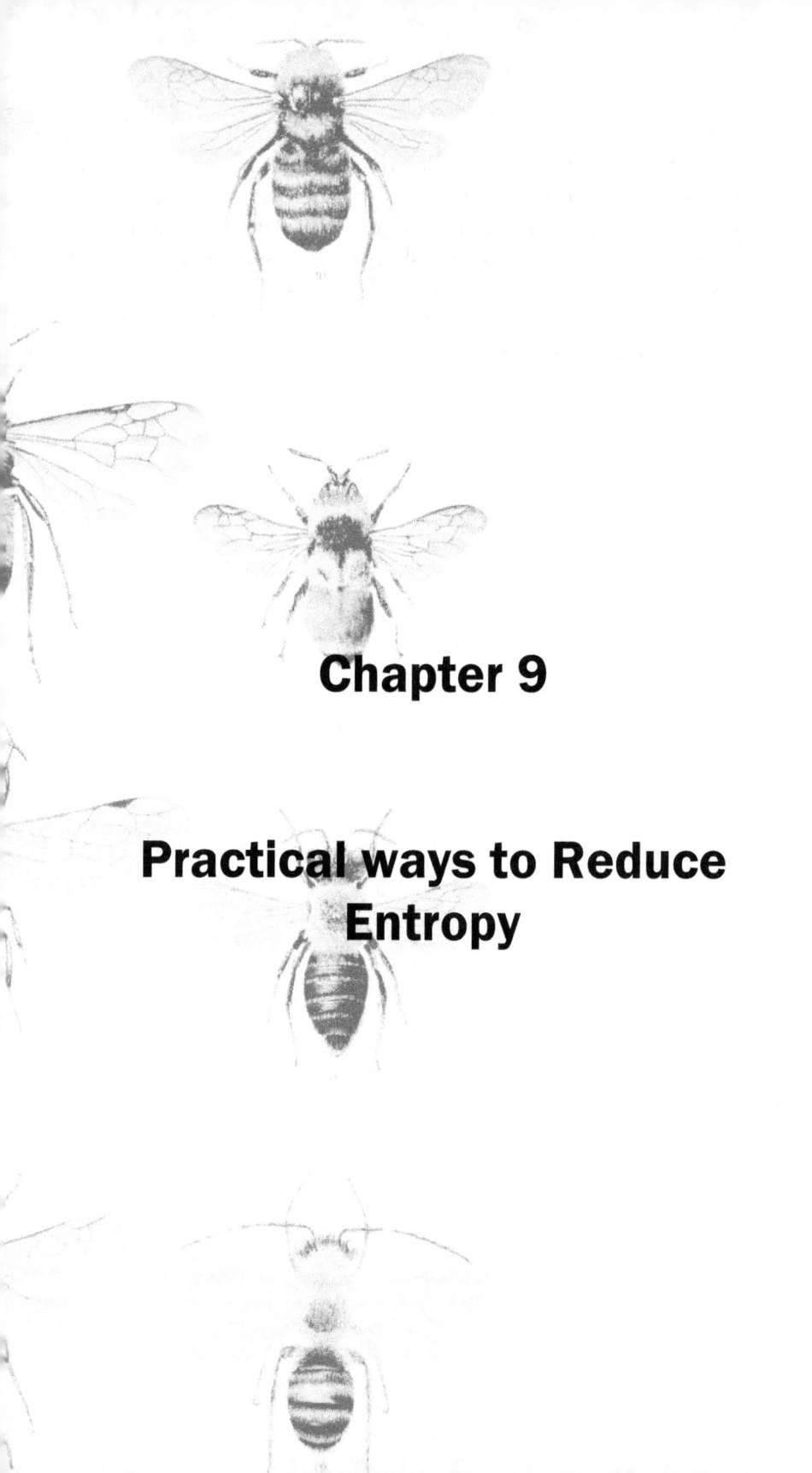

# Chapter 9

# Practical ways to Reduce Entropy

From personal experience I've created two fictional but representative retail chains, NovaWorld and Tradigo, as illustrative examples. At the start of the millennium, both were thriving with similar product offerings, comparable customer bases, and nearly identical operations. But when the digital age began to accelerate, their paths diverged dramatically.

NovaWorld chose to embrace the transformation systematically. NovaWorld's AI-powered inventory system enabled accurate prediction of seasonal demand patterns, allowing them to adjust staffing levels and product placement before rush periods hit. This predictive capability extended across the business as analytics identified purchasing patterns that substantially reduced inventory waste within the first year, while cloud-based dashboards gave local managers real-time visibility into sales trends for immediate responses to shifting customer preferences. Customer service shifted to intelligent chatbots that could resolve most inquiries instantly, with complex issues seamlessly escalated to human agents equipped with complete customer histories. Physical stores evolved into efficient fulfillment hubs where online orders could be ready for pickup within hours, transforming retail spaces from simple product displays into integrated service centers.

Tradigo, by contrast, maintained traditional operational methods despite shifting market dynamics. that had served them well for decades. Their inventory tracking relied on weekly paper reports that often arrived too late to prevent stockouts of popular items or overstock of slow-moving products. The basic company website functioned more like a digital brochure than a sales channel. Department managers operated in isolation, unaware of insights that neighboring sections had discovered about customer behavior. When supply chain disruptions emerged or consumer expectations shifted toward same-day delivery, Tradigo's response time stretched into weeks rather than days. Employees grew increasingly frustrated with tools that created more work instead of eliminating friction.

The choice wasn't between technology and tradition. It was between motion and stagnation, between clarity and confusion. In the end, only one of them was built for the future.

To survive entropy's relentless pull, companies must remain in motion, continuously applying energy not only to maintain structure but to adapt, evolve, and outpace changes that threaten disorder. The most effective approach begins with understanding which strategies deliver the greatest impact relative to their implementation difficulty.

The foundation of any entropy management effort rests on establishing clear communication channels and feedback systems, since these enable all other improvements. Companies should focus first on streamlining existing operations by identifying and eliminating redundant processes, as these changes typically show immediate results with minimal resource investment.

Innovation is the most vital source of organizational energy. A company that grows complacent risks watching its offerings, its services, even its internal processes drift toward obsolescence. But when a company commits itself to continuous invention, whether through research and development, exploration of emerging technologies, or simply nurturing a culture that refuses to accept the status quo, it maintains high energy reserves. New ideas fuel this process, ideas that spark fresh pathways and challenge conventional boundaries. It's not enough to passively acknowledge trends, companies must actively chase them, harness them, and reshape them into viable opportunities. Much like some technology firms, one we already looked at closely, that continuously refreshes their product portfolios, always venturing into new territories, seeking untapped markets or crafting novel solutions.

Not every shiny new pursuit guarantees success. A company must look toward the future, but not at the expense of what's thriving today. Innovation is vital, yet abandoning proven products and services in a rush to chase what might work tomorrow can become a costly distraction. Just as many organizations find better returns investing in their top performers rather than attempting to elevate underperformers, the same principle applies to focus. This is energy applied with purpose through focused work, and that's what keeps entropy at bay.

Alongside innovation, there's a quieter but equally important battle, the fight against internal complexity. Organizations naturally accumulate structural complexity over time. Layers of management multiply, decisions that once took hours begin to take days, and what was once a lean, nimble operation becomes bogged down by its own weight. A wise company recognizes this drift and acts before it calcifies. Streamlining operations becomes a vital form of work. By refining workflows, embracing automation, and digitizing systems, companies can return to a state of clarity. Think of a retail chain leveraging artificial intelligence to predict customer demand, eliminating inefficiencies that once led to stock shortages or surplus inventory. Every improvement, no matter how small, trims disorder from the system.

Once these foundational improvements stabilize, organizations can tackle more substantial challenges like digital transformation and innovation programs, which require greater energy investment but deliver proportionally higher returns. Of course, not all entropies arise from within. External forces, market shifts, technological revolutions, economic swings, continually exert pressure on organizational structures. Companies must keep their senses finely tuned to these changes, not merely reacting but anticipating. The businesses that thrive are those that treat external evolution as an invitation rather than a threat. Imagine a manufacturer of DVD players, once facing extinction, who sees the writing on the wall and boldly pivots toward streaming services or smart TV integrations. By redirecting their capacity and resources toward adaptation, they sidestep the fate of obsolescence.

But even more crucial than external awareness is the agility of the organization itself. An adaptable workforce is a living reservoir of energy. Flexibility happens not by accident but instead is cultivated by empowering teams to act swiftly, experiment freely, and collaborate seamlessly across boundaries. An organization that equips cross-functional teams with the autonomy to make fast decisions, moves like a school of fish, adjusting in unison to the currents of change, while their more cumbersome competitors lag behind, tangled in bureaucracy.

Leadership development and collaboration enhancement often run parallel to these efforts, building the organizational capacity needed to sustain momentum over time. Leadership plays an equally pivotal role in this effort. To sustain organizational energy over time, a company must invest in its people, not only hiring talent but nurturing it. Not only is the quality of your people important but so is filling the right leadership roles. As was pointed out brilliantly in *First, Break All the Rules* by Marcus Buckingham and Curt Coffman, the manager is the most important role in your company. As they put it so well, "People join companies, but they leave managers." It's not just a clever phrase; it's a critical insight. The daily experience of employees is not shaped by the CEO's vision but by their direct manager. To battle entropy, you need an amazing group of people who also understand what is at stake and are willing to fight alongside your chosen leadership. Training, mentorship, and the development of future leaders are not luxuries, they are necessities. An enterprise that equips its workforce with the skills to solve problems creatively, lead decisively, and adapt courageously, fortifies its energy reserves against entropy's advance. Through these efforts, the organization doesn't just react to change, it drives it. A brilliant innovation strategy, a flexible organizational structure, and a cutting-edge tech stack mean little if energy is being drained at the team level through unclear priorities, micromanagement, or a lack of psychological safety. The real question is whether your leaders are building capacity or burning it. Are you measuring their ability to develop talent, inspire progress, and reduce friction? Or are you overlooking one of the most immediate sources of entropy within your organization?

Energy flows best when shared, and collaboration becomes a powerful tool for reducing entropy. In open environments where ideas move freely, where teams challenge assumptions and engage in constructive dialogue, solutions often emerge from unexpected places. Companies that empower and support strong management can foster living systems capable of adjusting before disorder takes hold. Managers identify complexity early and address it before it spreads. Just as importantly, they create feedback loops that ask what's working, what's not, and how the system should evolve. This is why it is essential to understand whether a manager is adding value or needs support to become more effective. If the manager is the source of information feeding the feedback loop, but their insights are unreliable or biased, decisions will be made on flawed data. A strong culture of collaboration acts like a healthy immune system, catching dysfunction before it grows.

The most ambitious strategies, such as comprehensive cultural change and long-term sustainability initiatives, become viable only after the organization has proven its ability to execute focused improvements consistently. The companies that survive the longest are those that view their energy reserves not as resources to burn through hastily, but as capacity to conserve and deploy thoughtfully over time. Short-term wins might excite, but long-term vision sustains. Organizations that invest in sustainable practices, whether environmental, operational, or relational, build a reservoir of energy that slows entropy's march. A company that prioritizes renewable energy, fosters enduring partnerships, and resists the temptation of fleeting gains constructs a foundation that will last well beyond market cycles.

Embracing digital transformation is perhaps the most potent modern tool for holding entropy at bay. The smartest companies seize the advantages offered by new technologies, using them to refine production, automate repetitive tasks, predict future needs, and communicate with customers in real time. When digital tools are applied with precision, outdated systems fade away, replaced by efficient processes that hum with order and purpose. A company that integrates automation into its operations finds itself not merely surviving but thriving, as downtime diminishes and clarity reigns.

Digital transformation isn't just about adopting the latest tools; it's about reprogramming how the organization behaves. This is where Optidynamics intersects with modern operations by introducing well-designed systems that reduce entropy. Artificial intelligence, cloud infrastructure, and process automation aren't just conveniences; they are mechanisms that fight disorder. When digital processes are implemented with clarity and intent, they embed order into the company's DNA. Processes become traceable, data becomes connected, and decisions accelerate because insights arrive in real time. These are more than productivity gains, they are active entropy reducers. A digitally transformed company doesn't shy away from complexity; it makes complexity understandable. Forecasts become accurate through AI, bottlenecks vanish through automation, silos fall away with cloud-based collaboration. The result is a business with less friction and more flow, less chaos and more cohesion.

In the end, the story is simple but profound: entropy will always rise, but it can be fought. The company that chooses to innovate constantly, simplify its structures, adapt nimbly, invest in its people, encourage collaboration, pursue long-term sustainability, and embrace technology will not only endure, it will flourish. Optidynamics reminds us that energy isn't simply to be expended; it must be channeled through focused work. Success means the business remains vibrant, dynamic, and ready for whatever tomorrow brings.

Now that we've explored the practical methods to reduce entropy, it's important to remember that sometimes the most powerful strategy is not adding more energy but removing complexity altogether. Let's turn our attention to the timeless strength found in returning to simplicity.

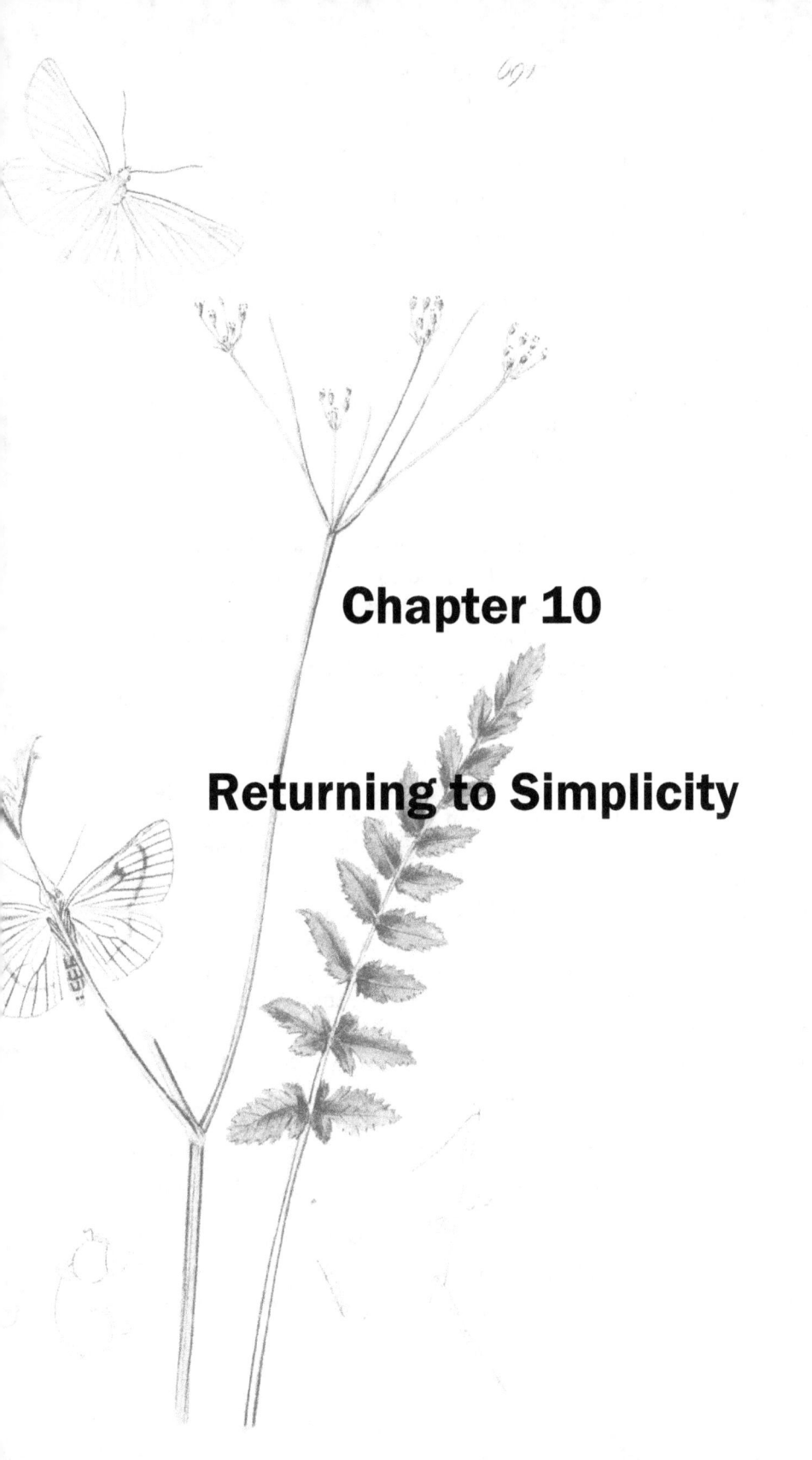

# Chapter 10

# Returning to Simplicity

Simplicity has become one of the most powerful tools a business can wield. When organizations become tangled in their own layers, whether through bloated processes, confusing communication structures, or redundant systems, they lose agility, they lose clarity. They lose the very energy they need to move forward.

Simplicity is not just about doing less. It's about doing less of what weakens the organization, leaving behind only the things that strengthen it. Constantly and deliberately stripping away anything that does not directly serve the mission. The end result is clarity of purpose, structure, and action.

As we discussed earlier, when a company is small, simplicity is natural. Decisions are made quickly. Problems are solved at the point of impact as they occur. There is little confusion about who is responsible for what. But as success builds, so too does the temptation to complicate things. Layers of process, multiple chains of command, and endless categories feel reasonable at first. Over time, the result is an organization that can barely move under its own weight.

Every decision, every meeting, and every project should be judged against a simple question: does this make the system more efficient, or does it make it heavier? Simplicity is not the absence of sophistication. Picture the expert sculptor chiseling away everything that is not the masterpiece, the goal is not to add but to reveal.

Companies that thrive over time understand that simplicity is a form of energy conservation. Every unnecessary meeting burns fuel. Every redundant approval layer leaks energy. Every confusing system bleeds momentum. Left unchecked, these small leaks accumulate until the organization becomes sluggish and vulnerable.

Toyota provides a powerful real-world example. By applying the philosophy of lean manufacturing, Toyota reduced waste, simplified production, and overtook competitors who relied on increasingly complex supply chains and assembly methods. The elegance of their system was not in its brilliance but in its relentless simplicity. Apple, too, famously succeeded by simplifying user experiences. While competitors loaded devices with endless features, Apple delivered products that focused only on what mattered, creating clarity for the user and reducing operational complexity internally. In both cases, simplicity was not a constraint. It was a competitive advantage.

Simplicity demands discipline. It requires leadership to protect it and fight the natural drift toward entropy that often masquerades as necessary progress. Every system that promises to streamline may secretly weave in new complexity. Every department created to manage change may inadvertently slow it down. The very departments formed to accelerate change often become the brakes. Without constant vigilance, organizations find themselves trapped in a cycle of patching inefficiencies with new layers of inefficiency, mistaking motion for progress while losing the very focus that fueled their rise.

The cultural cost of complexity is as real as the operational one. Confusing structures, unclear roles, and endless bureaucracy wear down the human spirit. Employees caught in the fog of complexity experience frustration, fatigue, and disengagement. Decisions take longer, creativity suffocates, and the quiet energy that once propelled a company forward drains away. Simplicity does not only make companies faster and more efficient, it also makes them happier, more humane places to work. A simple organization gives people room to think, space to act, and a shared sense of purpose that can be felt at every level.

Simplifying once is not sufficient. Simplicity is a continuous act, like tending to a bonsai tree, a rhythm of pruning and refining. You must adopt the habit of challenging assumptions, questioning whether processes still serve their purpose, and having the courage to remove what no longer does. Without this vigilance, complexity creeps back in through the cracks, disguised as innovation or strategic expansion, and entropy regains its foothold.

True simplicity is ruthless, but also honest. It does not disguise itself with new jargon or shiny rebranding. Beware of false simplicity, that is a clever trap where complexity is merely hidden rather than eliminated. A new platform that requires three layers of training is not simplification, even if it replaces five older systems. Real simplicity removes barriers. It does not merely rearrange them.

This is not to say that all complexity is inherently destructive. Certain types of complexity are not only unavoidable but essential for business growth and competitive advantage. A global supply chain requires sophisticated coordination mechanisms. Advanced manufacturing processes demand intricate quality control systems. Regulatory compliance in heavily regulated industries necessitates detailed procedures and documentation. The key distinction lies in understanding the difference between *necessary complexity* and *accumulated complexity*.

Necessary complexity serves a clear purpose and directly contributes to value creation or risk mitigation. When organizations choose to embrace this type of complexity, they must simultaneously increase their energy reserves and work capacity to manage the additional entropy it introduces. A pharmaceutical company developing life-saving drugs cannot avoid the complex regulatory framework, but it can invest heavily in specialized talent, robust project management systems, and streamlined approval processes to offset the inherent disorder. The complexity becomes manageable when the organization applies proportional energy to maintain clarity within that complexity.

The danger emerges when complexity accumulates without corresponding increases in organizational capability. This is entropy in its purest form: disorder that consumes energy without creating value. The art of leadership is recognizing which complexity serves the mission and which merely serves inertia.

The reward for simplicity is not only operational efficiency but with it, strategic clarity. The reward is the ability to see threats and opportunities clearly, to move quickly when conditions change, and to allocate energy where it has the greatest impact. In the language of Optidynamics, simplicity lowers entropy, sharpens focus, and ensures that energy is not wasted fighting the friction of a system that has forgotten its mission.

To return to simplicity is to return to strength. This is not regression, but instead refinement. The most enduring organizations are not those that accumulate the most but those that perfect the art of doing only what matters most. Returning to simplicity strengthens the foundation of any business, but simplicity alone is not enough. To truly master entropy, we must go beyond intuition and learn to measure chaos in order to see it clearly, track its growth, and apply energy precisely where needed. Let's now explore how to make entropy measurable and actionable.

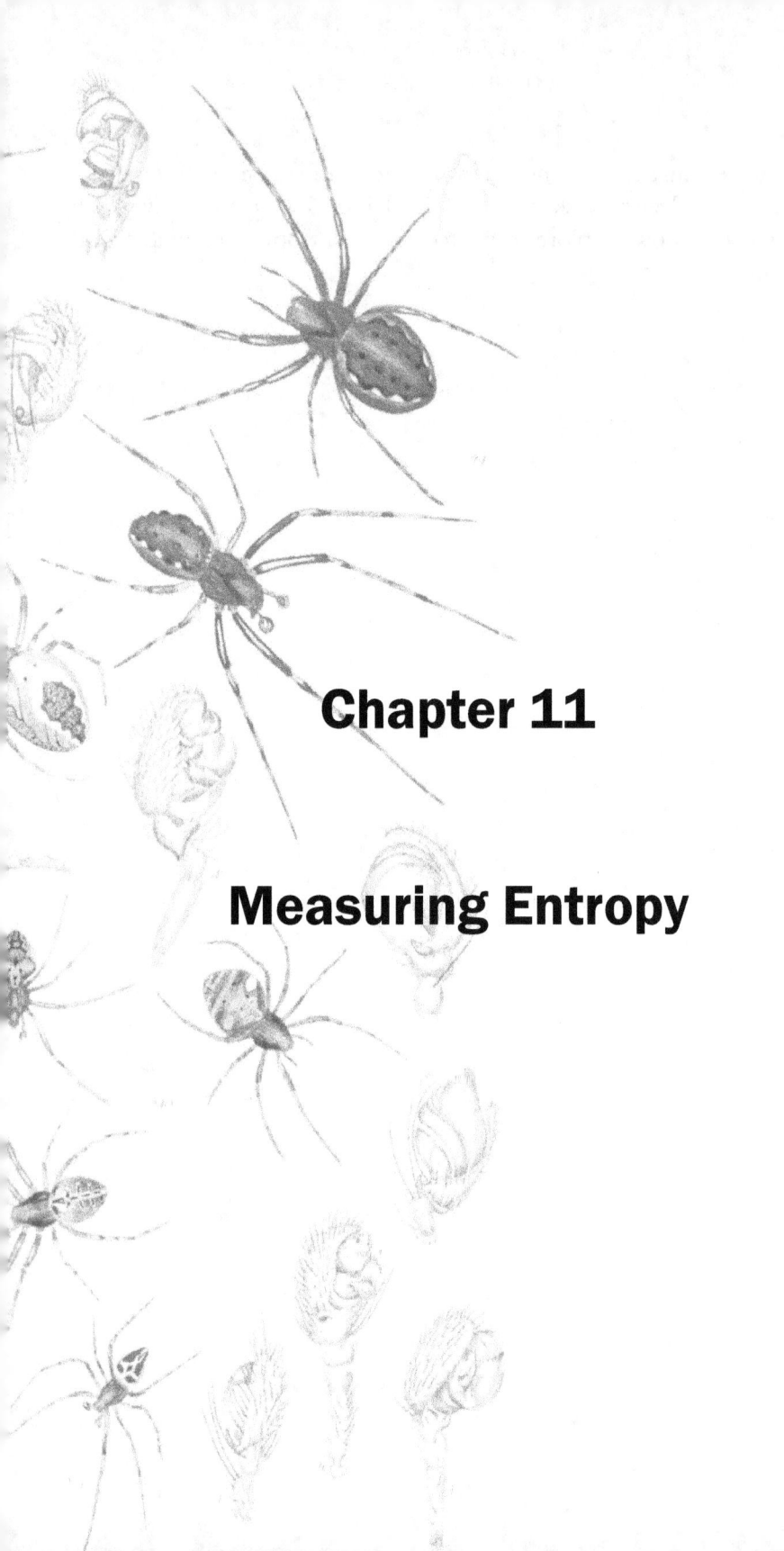

# Chapter 11

# Measuring Entropy

We have now built a new way of seeing how companies grow, falter, or thrive. We have explored the core forces of Optidynamics: energy, work, and entropy. These forces are not just abstract ideas. They are real and measurable inside any organization. Now let's take the next step, and turn our understanding into control.

Entropy is not some hidden mystery. It leaves fingerprints everywhere. It can be found in communication delays, slow decision-making, sagging energy, lost innovation, and creeping disorganization. Energy leaks out, work gets misdirected, alignment slips. Without a way to measure these patterns, companies drift without realizing it. When we can measure them, we can manage them. And when we can manage them, we can change the future.

To make this practical, we will break the system into the essential areas where these forces take shape: complexity, energy input, and structure. You already know them well from our journey so far. Complexity captures the tangled web of communication problems, decision-making delays, and operational sprawl that increase entropy. Energy input reflects the focused work and investment an organization makes to drive innovation, momentum, and progress. Structure represents the strength of leadership, the alignment of purpose, and the internal energy that keeps the system energized rather than cooling into stagnation.

These categories are broad by design, because your company isn't the same as anyone else's. The details of your business, your industry, your culture, and your market pressures are unique, but the forces of entropy apply to all of them. Let's take what we've learned, and use this framework to define your own specific, measurable indicators within each category. Look at the friction points in your organization. Where is energy being wasted? Where are decisions slow to be made? Where has complexity crept in unnoticed? Where is your work misaligned with your true goals?

If you instead are seeking a list of best practices, I have created suggestions of what I believe to be the top measurements in each category as well as a method for quantifying, baselining, measuring, and normalization. You can see these suggested metrics at Optidynamics.org.

Once you have defined your metrics you'll want to quantify these, because numbers tell the story over time. When you do, you'll also want to think about how much weight each metric deserves. Some areas of your business will carry more influence over entropy than others, decision-making speed, for instance, might matter more in a fast-moving tech startup than it does in a traditional manufacturing firm. Weighting allows you to respect those realities, giving the formula nuance and balance.

Finally, make sure you normalize your metrics. This is what brings everything onto the same playing field. Whether you're measuring in dollars, days, or percentages, normalizing lets you compare apples to apples. With all this in place you will be able to create an entropy score. This score should live cleanly between zero and one, as intended, making it easy to track over time and even compare across businesses one day, should you choose.

The act of building your entropy score is itself a discipline of clarity, forcing you to look closely at the machinery of your company and make the invisible visible. In doing so, you're already taking the most important step of recognizing entropy before it takes hold, and preparing to fight it with precision.

The first step toward clarity is transparency. Every metric, every data point, and every method of collection needs to be open to scrutiny. When numbers are tracked and shared with clear explanations of how they were gathered, the fog of bias begins to lift. Transparency not only builds trust across the organization, it also makes it far easier to spot errors or inconsistencies before they can do damage.

Collaboration across functions adds another layer of strength. When different departments work together to define key performance indicators, they bring diverse perspectives to the table. What one team views as a sign of order, another might see as creeping disorder. By involving voices from across the organization, you create a more balanced and accurate understanding of what truly constitutes entropy, work, and structure. This shared ownership of the measurement process helps to guard against blind spots that any single department might overlook.

There is also value in stepping outside the company entirely. Independent audits or third-party assessments provide an objective lens through which to view organizational complexity and performance. Without internal agendas at play, these evaluations can reveal truths that might otherwise remain hidden. They serve as a healthy check against internal bias, bringing fresh eyes to the intricacies of your operations.

Benchmarking offers another safeguard. By comparing your company's performance against industry standards and historical data, you ground your assessments in a broader context. This helps to minimize the influence of subjective interpretation, anchoring your metrics to external realities rather than internal perceptions alone.

Finally, establishing feedback loops keeps the process alive and responsive. Regular, honest conversations across departments ensure that progress is continuously validated and that adjustments are made as needed. These loops act as the company's internal compass, helping to course-correct before minor issues grow into significant problems. Building an Optidynamics working group will keep the improvements coming and the right kind of energy focused in the areas where the most chaos has the possibility to (or already has) entered your organization.

Reaching an accurate measurement of entropy is no easy task. As mentioned several times already, bias infiltrates measurement systems subtly, shaping how data is collected, how it is interpreted, and ultimately, how decisions are made. Stakeholders, often without even realizing it, bring their own interests and assumptions to the process. Left unchecked, these influences can cloud the results, leading to flawed conclusions and misguided actions. The challenge is real, but not insurmountable.

When these practices are woven together, they create a system that not only tracks entropy but does so with integrity. Collecting and analyzing these metrics consistently allows a company to see its entropy levels clearly, to understand the patterns beneath the surface, and to adjust its strategies with confidence. While no system is ever perfectly free from bias, a careful blend of transparency, collaboration, external review, benchmarking, and continuous feedback keeps bias in check and maintains the integrity of your insights.

In the end, managing entropy is more than simply running the numbers. Instead learn how to build a culture that respects the truth of those numbers, no matter how inconvenient they might be. With the right systems in place, you give your company the best chance not only to see disorder coming but to stop it before it takes hold.

Now that we can measure entropy and recognize where it threatens to grow into an uncontainable destructive force, it's time to move from observation to action. In the next section, you'll find a practical field guide with actual real-world strategies to apply Optidynamics and turn insight into momentum.

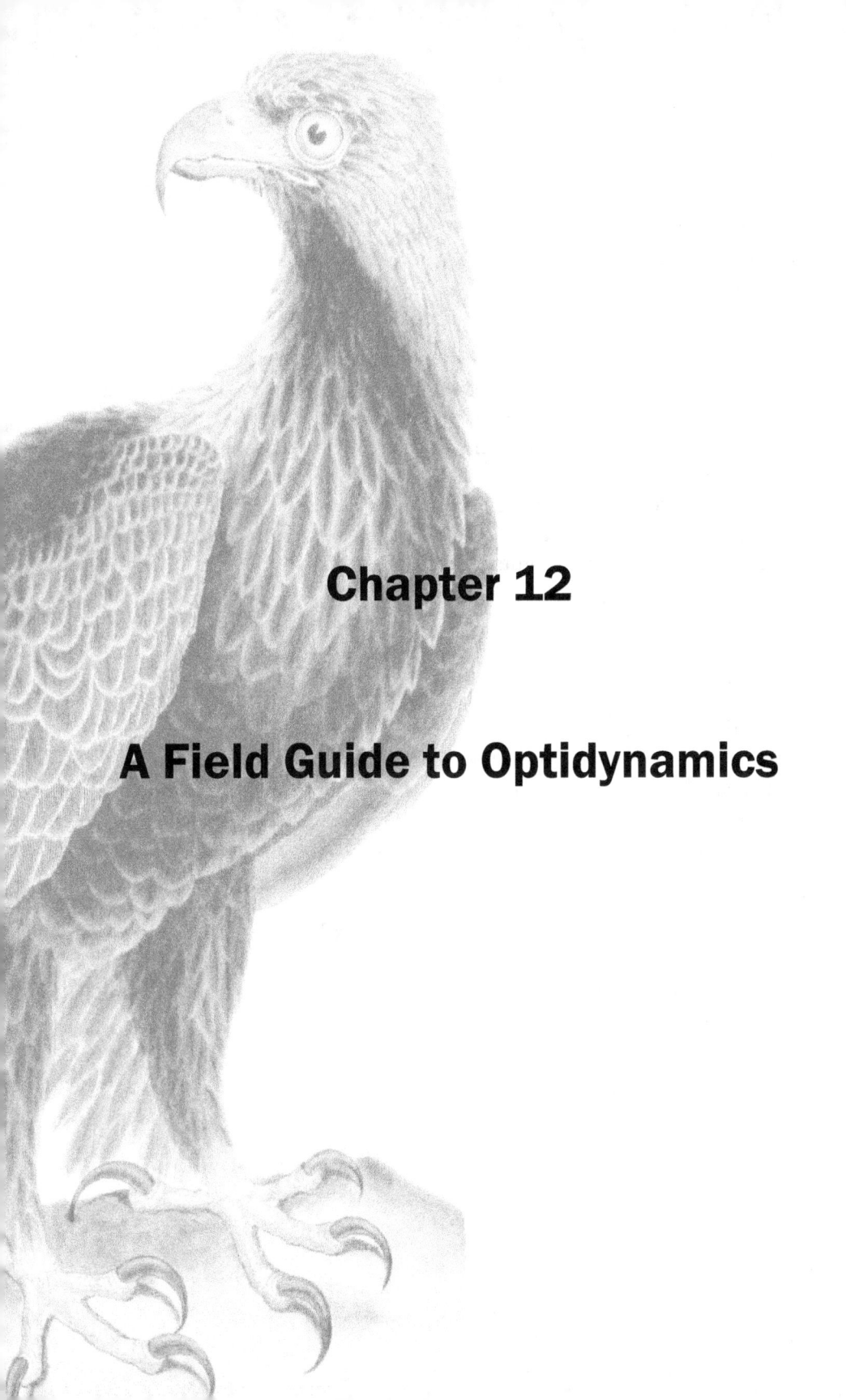

# Chapter 12

# A Field Guide to Optidynamics

You have now journeyed through the heart of Optidynamics, seen how companies soar, watched others stumble, and uncovered the hidden forces at work behind the scenes. You've learned to measure entropy and understand its patterns. Now it's time to give you something practical to carry into the field. This guide focuses not on birds or plants, but on the living patterns of entropy within your organization.

What follows is not another case study or theoretical framework. This is a practitioner's guide for identifying, diagnosing, and treating entropy in real-time business environments. Like any field guide, it's designed as a working reference tool with quick-access lists, diagnostic checklists, and structured information you can use while actively managing your organization. Like any well-worn field guide, the pages may bend and blur over time, but the insights it teaches will stay sharp. You'll learn to feel entropy shifting before it becomes visible and act before it becomes dangerous.

### How to Use This Guide

This field guide is designed for active use in your organizational environment. Keep it close when you're walking the halls, sitting in meetings, or reviewing project reports. Each section builds on the core Optidynamics principles you've learned, but organized for quick reference and practical application. When to Use This Guide:

- During project reviews when momentum feels off
- When teams seem to be spinning their wheels
- Before major organizational changes
- When communication patterns shift
- During periods of rapid growth or scaling

### Key Concepts Review:

- **Energy**: Available organizational capacity (talent, resources, capital, motivation)
- **Work**: Focused application of energy toward specific outcomes
- **Entropy**: Inefficiency, misalignment, and disorder that naturally increases over time
- **Entropy Score**: Your measured level of organizational disorder (0 to 1 scale)

*Quick Identification Keys*

# The Primary Entropy Assessment

Use these rapid questions to gauge your organization's entropy level: For a more detailed score card with weighting and standardization see www.Optidynamics.com

### Communication Clarity (Rate 0.0 to 1.0)

- Are decisions being made quickly and clearly?
- Do teams know what others are working on?
- Is important information reaching the right people?

### Energy Flow (Rate 0.0 to 1.0)

- Are people excited about their work?
- Do projects move forward with momentum?
- Is innovation happening organically?

### Structural Integrity (Rate 0.0 to 1.0)

- Are roles and responsibilities clear?
- Do processes help or hinder progress?

- Is leadership aligned and visible?

**Quick Diagnosis:**

- **0.0 to 0.3**: Low entropy, system is healthy
- **0.4 to 0.6**: Moderate entropy, monitor closely
- **0.7 to 1.0**: High entropy, immediate intervention needed

*Calculate your quick entropy score by averaging the three category ratings above.*

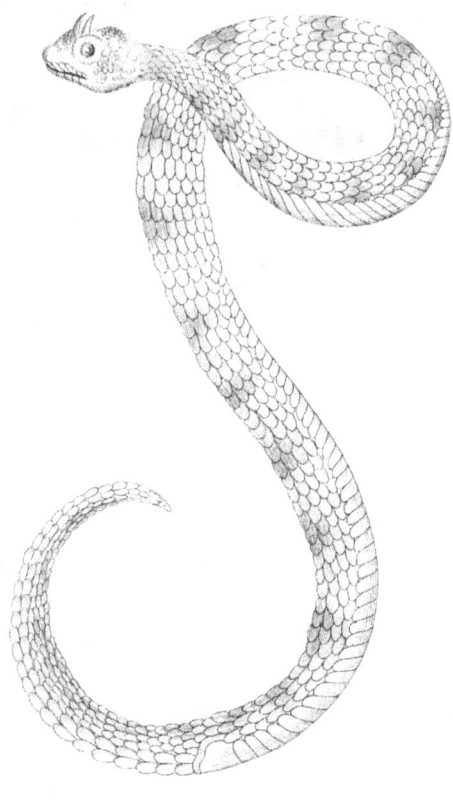

## Warning Sign Taxonomy

### Category A: Communication Breakdown

- Messages scattered or unclear
- Longer meetings with less clarity
- Information trapped in silos
- Decisions take longer than before

### Category B: Energy Depletion

- Projects stalling without clear cause
- Team enthusiasm cooling
- Innovation becoming rare
- "We've always done it this way" mindset

### Category C: Structural Decay

- Role confusion increasing

- Process proliferation
- Leadership becoming defensive
- Bureaucracy over action

## *Species Accounts: Common Entropy Manifestations*

## The Analysis Paralysis Syndrome

**Identifying Features:** Endless research phases, multiple draft versions never finalized, meeting after meeting without decisions, perfectionism masquerading as thoroughness.

**Habitat:** Commonly found in strategic planning committees, product development teams, and academic-oriented organizations.

**Behavior Patterns:** Feeds on uncertainty and fear of failure. Grows stronger when timelines are loose and accountability is unclear.

**Treatment:** Apply completion deadlines, embrace "good enough" standards, focus on iteration over perfection. Remember the insight that inspired Optidynamics: "It's better than good, it's done."

**Similar Species:** Perfectionism Paralysis (distinguished by quality obsession rather than analysis obsession)

## The Bureaucratic Bloat

**Identifying Features:** Multiplication of approval layers, forms for requesting forms, committees to discuss forming committees, process documentation that exceeds actual work effort.

**Habitat:** Large established organizations, regulated industries, any company experiencing rapid growth without structural pruning.

**Behavior Patterns:** Self-perpetuating. Each inefficiency creates a perceived need for more oversight, which creates more inefficiency.

**Treatment:** Process audits focused on value creation, elimination of redundant approvals, empowerment of decision-makers at the front lines.

**Similar Species:** Red Tape Infestation (government specific variant), Policy Proliferation (distinguished by document quantity over process complexity)

## The Silo Syndrome

**Identifying Features:** Departments protecting information, competing rather than collaborating, duplicated efforts across teams, "not my department" attitudes.

**Habitat:** Organizations with unclear shared goals, competitive internal cultures, or poorly designed incentive structures.

**Behavior Patterns:** Territorial marking through information hoarding, resource guarding, blame deflection during problems.

ɔjectives across departments, cross-functional project teams, celebration of collaborative victories.

**Similar Species:** Turf War Disorder (more aggressive variant), Knowledge Hoarding Habit (typically individual rather than departmental behavior)

## The Innovation Drought

**Identifying Features:** Risk aversion, reliance on "proven methods," dismissal of new ideas, stagnant product development, competitive position eroding.

**Habitat:** Successful companies becoming complacent, heavily regulated industries, leadership focused on preserving rather than growing.

**Behavior Patterns:** Feeds on comfort and fear of change. Often accompanied by defensive justifications of current state.

**Treatment:** Innovation time allocation, experimentation budgets, failure tolerance policies, external perspective injection.

**Similar Species:** Complacency Creep (broader organizational issue), Change Resistance (more active opposition to new methods)

## The Communication Chaos

**Identifying Features:** Important information gets lost, wrong people in meetings, right people missing from decisions, conflicting messages from leadership.

**Habitat:** Typically lives in fast-growing organizations, remote teams without clear protocols, companies undergoing structural changes.

**Behavior Patterns:** Thrives in unclear hierarchies and ambiguous communication channels. Multiplies during periods of change.

**Treatment:** Clear communication hierarchies, standardized information flows, regular alignment check-ins.

**Similar Species:** Information Overload (too much communication rather than poor communication), Message Fragmentation (content quality vs. delivery quality issues.

*Diagnostic Procedures*

## The Five-Minute Entropy Scan

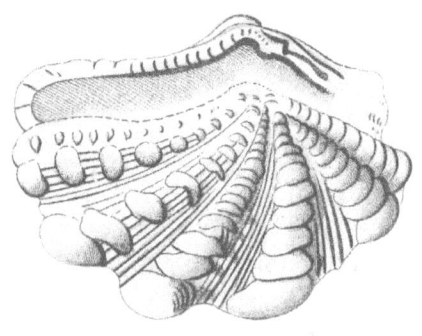

When you sense something is off but can't pinpoint it:

1.  **Listen to the language**: Are people saying "we should" or "we will"? Future tense often indicates there is stalled energy.

2.  **Observe the meeting dynamics**: Who's talking? Who's checking out? Energy flows are visible in engagement patterns.

3.  **Check the project momentum**: What's the time between decision and action? Growing delays signal increasing entropy.

4.  **Feel the emotional temperature**: Frustration, confusion, and resignation are entropy's most telling calling cards.

5.  **Look for work around patterns**: When people consistently bypass official processes, entropy has made those processes ineffective.

## The Deep Entropy Assessment

For systematic organizational health checks:

### Week 1: Shadow Normal Operations

- Attend regular meetings as observer
- Track decision to action timelines
- Take note of informal communication patterns
- Document frustration points

### Week 2: Energy Flow Mapping

- Always identify where enthusiasm is high and low
- Find innovation sources and blockers
- Map resource allocation vs. results
- Assess leadership visibility and clarity

### Week 3: Structural Analysis

- Review process efficiency
- Examine role clarity across teams
- Evaluate feedback loop effectiveness
- Test information flow accuracy

### Week 4: Synthesis and Action Planning

- Calculate entropy scores using your metrics
- Identify highest impact intervention points
- Design energy injection strategies
- Establish monitoring systems

### *Treatment Protocols*

# Emergency Interventions (High Entropy, Score 0.7 and above)

### Immediate Actions:

- Leadership alignment session
- Project triage, make kill, continue, or postpone decisions
- Communication channel simplification
- Quick win identification and execution

### Week 1 Follow up:

- Daily stand ups across affected areas
- Obstacle removal task force
- Clear success metrics establishment
- Regular entropy monitoring

## Preventive Maintenance (Moderate Entropy, Score 0.4 to 0.6)

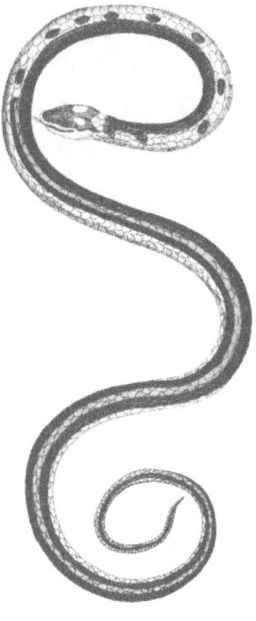

### Monthly Practices:

- Process efficiency reviews
- Cross functional collaboration check-ins
- Innovation pipeline assessment
- Leadership visibility rounds

### Quarterly Practices:

- Organizational structure evaluation
- Communication effectiveness surveys
- Energy source identification and renewal
- Long term vision realignment

## Ongoing Health (Low Entropy, Score 0.0 to 0.3)

### Continuous Practices:

- Cultural norm reinforcement
- Proactive complexity management
- Regular system optimization
- Future entropy threat assessment

*Field Notes Section*

## Common Misdiagnoses

**Mistake:** Assuming low energy means lazy people **Reality:** Often indicates unclear direction or blocked processes

**Mistake:** Thinking more communication solves communication problems **Reality:** Usually requires clearer, simpler communication channels

**Mistake:** Adding processes to fix process problems **Reality:** Typically requires process elimination and simplification

## Seasonal Patterns

**Growth Phases:** Entropy naturally increases during expansion, normal but requires active management

**Crisis Periods:** Entropy can temporarily decrease as organization focuses, but rebounds quickly without conscious effort

**Success Periods:** Highest entropy risk due to complacency and complexity creep

## Field Equipment Recommendations

- Regular entropy measurements (your custom metrics)
- Anonymous feedback channels
- Process mapping tools
- Decision timeline tracking
- Energy source identification methods

*Advanced Identification Techniques*

## Reading Organizational Body Language

Organizations, like people, show stress through subtle signs:

**Healthy Organization Signals:**

- Quick, casual information sharing
- Natural collaboration across boundaries
- Problems addressed promptly and openly
- Experimentation and calculated risk taking
- Leadership is accessible and responsive

## Entropy Warning Signals:

- Formal communication replacing informal
- Increased meeting frequency with decreased decisions
- Blame assignment becoming common
- Innovation suggestions dismissed quickly
- Leadership becoming isolated or defensive

**Entropy Velocity Assessment**

Not just how much entropy exists, but how fast it's growing:

**Stable Entropy:** Problems exist but aren't worsening **Accelerating Entropy:** Problems multiplying and compounding **Critical Entropy:** System approaching breakdown

**Measurement Technique:** Track your entropy metrics over 4 week periods. Plot the rate of change, not just the absolute values.

### *Conclusion: The Practice of Entropy Management*

This field guide is not a checklist to be completed once and forgotten. It's a companion to carry with you. Every company, every project, every idea you will ever build will dance with entropy. That is the natural law. Your role, as a dynamic leader, is not to fear this dance but to master it.

Stay alert to the signs. Don't ignore what your metrics and your eyes are telling you. Diagnose carefully where the disorder is forming. Apply energy with focus and speed. Reinforce clarity, rekindle purpose, engineer collaboration, renew leadership. Move constantly but move wisely.

You cannot eliminate entropy forever. But you can outwork it, outthink it, and outlast it longer than anyone who stands still. That is the path of Optidynamics. That is the way great companies endure.

Remember, this is your guide, not your destination. Like any experienced naturalist, you'll develop sharper eyes for patterns unique to your environment. Mark up these pages. Add your own observations. Cross out what doesn't apply and highlight what proves most useful. The best field guides become deeply personal tools, shaped by the wisdom of real experience.

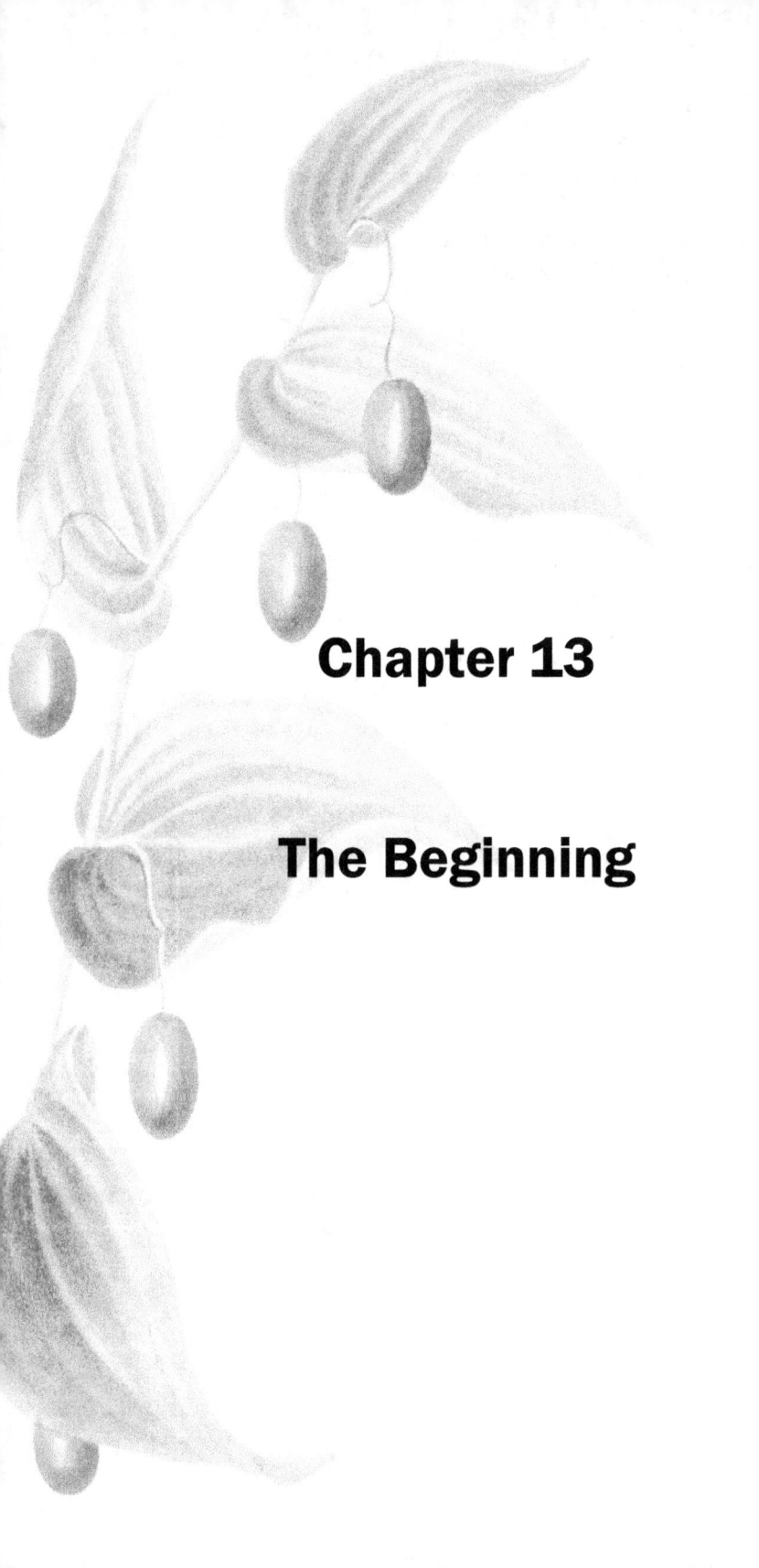

# Chapter 13

# The Beginning

Every business, like any complex system, wrestles daily with the quiet but relentless pull of entropy. It is not something you see at first. It gathers slowly in the background, a subtle drift toward disorder. Processes grow tangled, teams fall out of alignment, and decisions take longer to reach. Left unattended, these small inefficiencies compound until they weigh down even the most promising enterprises. Optidynamics takes the universal law of thermodynamics and reframes it, giving us not just a way to understand the forces at play, but a way to control them.

This is not simply about surviving chaos. It is about knowing where to channel energy, how to build structures that endure, and how to keep organizations fluid enough to thrive no matter how the environment shifts. Every great company begins as a tight, energetic force, burning brightly with purpose and momentum. But as success builds, so does complexity. Without vigilance, what began as an agile, focused endeavor can slowly become heavy with layers of process and inertia. Optidynamics provides the framework to anticipate this, to measure it, and to fight it with precision.

What makes this approach so powerful is that it does not remain locked in theory. It lives in action. We have explored the mechanics, from complexity to energy input to structure, and we have seen how these elements can be measured, adjusted, and improved. We have examined real companies, some that faltered under entropy's weight, and others that found ways to rise again. These stories show us that success is not just about weathering today's storms, but about building a vessel strong enough to navigate the currents of tomorrow, and the tomorrows after that.

And the possibilities reach far beyond the boardroom. Because energy and entropy are universal forces, they shape every kind of organization, not just corporations. The same patterns shape governments, non-profits, communities, even personal productivity. Any system that seeks to grow, evolve, and endure must contend with the same forces. By applying Optidynamics beyond business, we open doors to smarter cities, more effective organizations, and lives designed with intentionality and resilience. The potential is vast.

At its core, Optidynamics is a reminder that longevity is not a matter of luck, it is a craft. Companies that stand the test of time do not succeed by chance. They succeed by choice, by staying in motion, by constantly rebalancing and refining how they apply their energy. Heraclitus captured it well when he observed that: "No man steps into the same river twice, because both the man and the river are always changing."

In simplest terms, change is life's only constant. Optidynamics does not ask us to resist this truth, but to work with it. To understand it. To turn it from a threat into an ally. When we do, we unlock the ability to shape not only the future of our businesses, but perhaps, in some small way, the future itself. It is the practice of applying energy intentionally to counteract complexity, sustain momentum, and keep systems in motion.

Afterword: A Personal Note

Thank you for taking this journey with me.

Optidynamics began as a simple observation, a thread of thought that kept pulling at me over the years. I had seen it too many times. Great ideas left unrealized, promising companies drifting into disorder, energy wasted where it could have been harnessed. It always came back to the same question, why do some businesses thrive while others, equally capable, slowly lose their way?

Writing this book has been a way of answering that question, not just for myself, but for anyone who has ever built something and wondered how to keep it alive and well. The patterns are universal. The forces of energy, work, and entropy do not care what industry you are in or how big your ambitions are. It applies to us all, whether we recognize it or not.

But recognition is power. By seeing these forces clearly, by measuring them and responding with intent, you have the ability to steer your organization toward endurance, toward clarity, and toward resilience. Optidynamics is not a guarantee of success, but instead a solid blueprint for giving your best ideas their strongest possible chance to survive and thrive.

I hope this framework serves you well, not just in business, but in any system you choose to build. If this book has helped you look at your company a little differently, given you a new lens to see challenges and opportunities, or simply sparked a new conversation in your mind, then it has done its job.

This is not the end of the journey. Like any living system, Optidynamics will continue to evolve, and so will you. I look forward to seeing where you take it.

Stay curious, stay energized, and most of all, stay in motion.

-   Steve

# OPTIDYNAMICS

# APPENDIX

Steve Bevilacqua, author and founder of Optidynamics, is available for keynotes, workshops, and executive advisory engagements. He turns the ideas in this book into practical methods your team can apply immediately, with clear priorities, faster delivery, and simple ways to measure progress.

For availability, booking, and supplemental materials please visit Optidynamics.org

**Artistic Credit**

All artwork is used with permission and thanks from the Biodiversity Heritage Library

https://blog.biodiversitylibrary.org/
https://www.flickr.com/photos/biodivlibrary/albums/

Intro - Transactions of the Zoological Society of London v.17 (1903-1906) London: Published for the Zoological Society of London by Academic Press

Chapter 1 - Deutschlands flora in abbildungen nach der natur Nurnberg: Gedruckt auf kosten des verfassers, 1798-[1862]

Chapter 2 - The royal natural history London: F. Warne, 1893-1896

Chapter 3 - The spiders of the United States Boston: Boston Society of Natural History, 1875

Chapter 4 - Atlas der baumarten von Java Lieden: Buch- und Steindruckerei, 1913-18

Chapter 5 - The mineral conchology of Great Britain London: Printed by B. Meredith [etc.], 1812-[1846]

Chapter 6 - Vilmorin's Blumengärtnerei Berlin: P. Parey, 1896

Chapter 7 - Icones Bogorienses v.1 (1897-1901) Leiden: E. J. Brill, 1897-1914

Chapter 8 - Des Ritters Carl von Linné ... Vollständiges Natursystem: nach der zwölften lateinischen Ausgabe, und nach Anleitung des holländischen Houttuynischen Werks, mit einer ausführlichen Erklärung Th.6:Bd.1

Chapter 9 - Report, State Entomologist of Minnesota to the Governor 17th (1918) St. Paul, Minn.: Agricultural Experiment Station

Chapter 10 - British entomology v.6 London: Printed for the author, 1823-1840 [i.e. 1840]

Chapter 11 - A history of the spiders of Great Britain and Ireland London: Published for the Ray Society by Robert Hardwicke, 1861-1864

Chapter 12 - Planches enluminées d'histoire naturelle t.5 Paris: s.n., 1765-1783

Getreue Abbildungen naturhistorischer Gegenstände in Hinsicht auf Bechsteins kurzgefasste gemeinnützige Naturgeschichte des In- und Auslandes: für Eltern, Hofmeister, Jugendlehrer, Erzieher und Liebhaber der Naturgeschichte, Bd.6 (1793) Nürnberg: In der Schneider und Weigelschen Kunst- und Buch- handlung, [1793-1809]

Chapter 13 - Wild flowers of Nova Scotia Halifax, N.S.: Published by C.H. Belcher, and J. Snow, London, 1840-1853

www.ingramcontent.com/pod-product-compliance
Lightning Source LLC
Chambersburg PA
CBHW070303290526
45791CB00003B/1071